RAISING
BLUE-COLLAR KIDS IN
A WHITE-COLLAR WORLD

RAISING BLUE-COLLAR KIDS IN A WHITE-COLLAR WORLD

Toughening Up Your Kids with
GRIT & GRACE

By

CONOR GALLAGHER

A Well-Ordered Family Short Read

Unless otherwise noted, Scripture quotations are from the Revised Standard Version of the Bible—Second Catholic Edition (Ignatius Edition), copyright © 2006 National Council of the Churches of Christ in the United States of America. Used by permission. All rights reserved.

Cover & interior design by David Ferris, www.davidferrisdesign.com

ISBN: 978-1-5051-3631-9

Published in the United States by
TAN Books
PO Box 269
Gastonia, NC 28053

Printed in the United States of America

To Aiden and Patrick—my first two sons,
who have blue-collar souls in very different
but equally beautiful ways.

CONTENTS

INTRODUCTION

Dear Reader,

It used to be prestigious just to go to college. But now, a college degree is given the accolades that a high school degree used to command. That is, of course, unless you attend an elite college.

Statistically, if your kid attends a so-called "elite" college, he is likely to lose his faith, become Pro-Choice, graduate as a communist-leaning socialist, and adopt woke ideology. Highbrow education seems to have sucked common sense right out of multiple generations of Americans.

But this little book isn't about elitist ideology. It is about the elitist soul, which is far worse than bad ideology. An elitist soul is one that feels entitled, that expects to consume rather than to produce, that expects experts to handle the hard work, and that feels "above" the dirty work.

Any employer, like myself, who has been trying to staff his company in the last ten years has seen a massive shift from previous years. We have a new generation of college graduates demanding grossly high salaries, accommodations for every possible scenario, and the assumption that they can work from home. Perhaps worse than anything is that the crop of new workers are, in my experience, completely incapable of dealing with criticism, push back, or authority in general. Yes, we have fully entered into the Age of Entitlement.

While a good salary and remote work can be a worthy goal and, of course, formal education is a beautiful thing, we have lost something vital as a society, and that is grit. *Grit*. So often in my own business I have seen young people clutching their expensive university diplomas, bewildered that they're not six-figure salary managers. They are shocked that **gasp** they have to work in the office and interact with a team.

This age of entitlement has brainwashed many poor souls into thinking that they deserve the fruits of labor without ever putting in a full day's work in the vineyard. In reality, the young adults are not to blame. Frankly, I think their parents are to blame. They raised spoiled and entitled children, no matter the household income.

What I've come to realize, and what this little book explores, is that the most successful people in history, whether its presidents, business tycoons, or saints, all had one thing in common: grit.

While their outward appearance may have the luster of white-collar success, their souls remained blue-collar, which is to say, they never lost the drive to get their hands dirty, to work tirelessly toward something good—not for any lauds or rewards, but because they learned that hard work isn't just a means to an end, but that it can be the end in itself.

As parents, your goal is to get your kids to heaven. By helping them to form the virtue of grit, which is the ability to persevere, to possess grace under pressure, to have true longanimity, you not only provide them a platform from which to remain steady amid the storms of life but also give them the inner strength to push themselves to their fullest God-given potential.

Dear parents: teach your children to do things themselves, to get in the mud and get dirty, to learn as much as possible in those moments of suffering. If you do so, you can give your kids the chance to become who they were meant to be. But if they lack the virtue of grit, they will never endure long enough to find their true potential.

No parent wishes undo suffering on his child, no parent wishes his child to fail or fall into despair. But these things are realities of life. Suffering will happen. But how you prepare them to face these trials now will make all the difference. Handouts without consequence, handling everything for them, pacifying them with screens so you can clean their messes—this is not parenting. This is cutting their legs from under them.

Once your child is out in the world, having to discern his life, having to make decisions between right and wrong, what will they do? Do you trust your child to rise up and face those challenges? To remain morally straight and embrace what the world throws at them with grit and grace? Or will they run and hide and complain about the unfairness of the world?

Of course, you wish your children to have good jobs and great families and to be met with success in life. But no amount of coddling will prepare them. It takes hard work. In fact, a blue-collar spirit will help their white-collar career more than anything.

And this is the point of this little book. Your kid doesn't need to be a mechanic or farmer or plumber. They can strive to be the head of tech start-up or doctor or the president. None of that matters. The only thing that matters is the state of their soul. And a blue-collar soul is what will guide them through suffering and defeat, and get them to that luminous other side: grace.

So, dear parents, are you ready to help your children develop grit? Are you ready to help them reach their fullest potential? Are you ready to help them become saints? Then read on and we will explore how to raise your kids to develop a blue-collar soul in a white-collar world.

—Conor Gallagher

YOU HAVE

THE MORAL DUTY

TO TEACH YOUR CHILD

TO SUFFER WELL

DITCHING THE WHITE-COLLAR MINDSET

What is a blue-collar kid? Or better yet, what does it mean to raise a kid with a blue-collar soul? It has nothing to do with one's career or how much money one makes. It has nothing to do with status in society or one's intelligence. Someone with a blue-collar soul is in fact rather ordinary, and this, most especially in today's world, makes them extraordinary. It begins with clearing your soul of the world's dust, which falls like glitters of gold flaking off the golden calf of the white-collar world. It begins with emptying oneself of pride and sloth. In regard to our kids, it begins with helping them avoid pride and sloth. In short, it begins with humility and grit for you and me, your kids and my kids.

This, dear parents, is the blue-collar soul. And this book is my explanation of why you need to raise your kids to have a blue-collar soul in a white-collar world.

THE STORY OF A PRESIDENT

When I was a child, my dad told me a story about Ronald Reagan that I've never forgotten.

During his presidency, Reagan was often described as the most powerful man in the world. And yet, the president was shockingly humble and modest. Vice President George H.W. Bush recalled experiencing this when he went to visit him in the hospital after the 1981 attempted assassination of Reagan. The visit stuck with the vice president long after.

As he entered the hospital room, the vice president saw that Reagan wasn't lying in his bed. He looked around and almost left when the familiar voice said, "Hello, George." The vice president turned to find Reagan on his hands and knees in the bathroom. "Are you all right, Mr. President?" Bush asked. Reagan smiled and explained that he had spilled some water and was wiping it up. "I don't want the nurses to have to mop it up," he said. "I'm enough of a nuisance to them as it is. Be with you in a second." Bush later stated in an interview, "That's the sort of man Ronald Reagan was."

Now, this is a perfect example of humility and modesty, two virtues I've tried to practice every day. But more so, this is an example of a man who had a blue-collar soul and mindset. This is what we must teach our children to become.

"There are no easy answers, but there are simple answers. We must have the courage to do what we know is morally right."

–Ronald Reagan

In the simplest way, it begins with humility. In this anecdote from President Reagan's life, we see a man who had the whitest collar job possible—he wouldn't need to lift a finger to do anything if he didn't wish, and no one would blink an eye or judge him for it. And yet, there he was doing one of the most humble things ever—cleaning up a bathroom floor.

Now, this may seem inconsequential to you, it may seem like a nice thought but has no bearing on real life. But if you can't see the beauty in this story, then close the book now. Let me ask you this, dear parents: If your kid is president, will he clean up his own spill so the maid doesn't have to?

This is at the heart of the matter concerning our children and society today. We've lost something very important as we've gained and acquired so much trash. We've forgotten what it means to live humbly, to push ourselves out of comfort and into something far better. We've become afraid of real, hard work, and we've tried to spare our children such hard work as well. We've exchanged grit for comfort. But the harsh truth is that by giving your kid everything, you're taking everything away.

THE 40% RULE

Retired U.S. Navy SEAL Dave Goggins developed what is now known as the "40% rule." This he learned during his training and career as a SEAL. Goggins' rule states that when you think you've reached your limit or think you're done, you're actually only 40% done, and you still have 60% left in the tank.

This rule is another example demonstrating the essence of a blue-collar soul: they understand hard work, they know that when they've reached a perceived limit, they still have more to go.

Your kids need to understand this. They need to understand that when they first encounter an obstacle it is usually, by nature, an easy limit to overcome. Things become hard progressively. Thus, a small amount of effort never

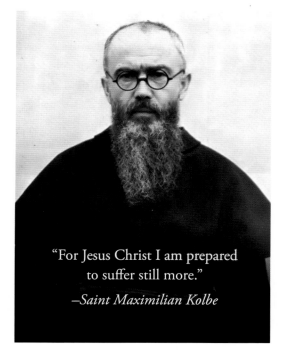

"For Jesus Christ I am prepared to suffer still more."

—*Saint Maximilian Kolbe*

encounters a high degree of difficulty. Tough people know this. They know that suffering is endured for a good deal of time before they overcome it. But the wimp? The first sign of difficulty cripples them. They confuse it with a true limit, an immovable object, a barrier they are unable to scale, a suffering they are unable to endure. By developing the virtue of fortitude, or perseverance, one's threshold for suffering grows and grows and grows. It's not unlike the very first time you stretch and try to reach your toes. It hurts that first time, but you know the more you try, the farther you will reach. But if you quit at that first sign of pain, at the first pangs of suffering, you will never know the fruits of what lies beyond. Your job as parents is to help your kids push beyond those perceived limits.

Hear me, Christian Parent: *you* have a grave moral duty to teach your child to suffer well.

Perceived limits are at an all-time low in this society because of our age of comfort, leisure, and commercialism. Children are being pacified to such sad extremes. Especially when both parents have to work, it's often easier to give the kids what they want to make the suffering pass. We give them technology, we give them crappy food, we comply and compromise with tantrums. In one sense, the super busy parents are pacifying their children to make their own life easier. Do you realize how hard it is to make your kids do their chores? Sometimes it's easier for me to just do the darn chore than getting the kids to do it.

But remember, dear parent: Thou shalt not rob thy kids of the moral fruit of doing their chores.

STRONG PARENTS CREATE STRONG KIDS

In our complicated modern world, there's nothing wrong *per se* with two working parents. These days, it's extremely difficult to maintain a single income household. But when both parents are working what can easily happen is that your kids are forgotten and left to their own devices. They're pacified with T.V., video games, endless sports practices, etc., because mom and dad are busy. This can also happen with a mom or dad who's at home but are lazy. You can have lazy parents whether they're working or not. Parents can be home all day and still spoil their kids because they're not truly engaged with them. In essence, it becomes this dynamic of: It's just easier for me to do the dishes myself. It's just easier for me to clean the playroom. It's easier for me to cut the grass than to teach my teenager how to do it. It's easier for me to do these things because training a child in the art and science of life is a very difficult, demanding, and frustrating activity.

More likely, however, is the dynamic where you fear making your kid work hard. You fear them revolting against you. I see this all the time. Parents can't communicate tough lessons because the teenager might say, "Whatever man! I'm out!" Is your relationship with your son and daughter not strong enough to withstand a little discomfort? The irony is that strong parents who deliver strong messages create strong bonds with their kids. Weak parents who can't deliver strong messages create weak bonds.

Here is the self-fulling prophesy:
your fear of ruining the relationship ruins the relationship.

I am teaching my kid how to drive right now and, honestly, I hate doing it. Driving myself is much easier. But if you're a parent who has a 15-year-old with a driver's permit, you have a moral duty to make them drive as much as possible before they get their license. No matter what. When I'm in a hurry and I want to get somewhere I have to take a deep breath and make him drive. When it's pouring rain and I'm nervous about him driving, I have to make him drive so that he learns. I have to make the painstaking effort, which I hate doing, and make him drive. Why? Because I have to use all of those opportunities to train him to be a good driver before he gets in the car by himself. There is a moral duty to maximize that time and train your kids. Parents that let their kids get a driver's permit and never get in the car with them, never teach them, are morally incompetent. Lives are at stake, and soon their kid is on the highway, driving through town, completely unprepared.

This same dynamic of actively teaching your kids must be applied with chores, with yard work, with learning how to fix things, with developing relationships. You must teach them. It takes selflessness to make your kids do stuff for themselves. When parents in today's world are so overwhelmingly busy with their own careers and social life and social media, they end up pacifying their children to make their own life easier. Suddenly, kids aren't taught even the basics of how to be an adult, of how to be a part of a family or community. At the slightest notion of work or chores, kids throw tantrums and parents compromise, making the moment easier, and the future much harder.

This is where the 40% rule can really help. It is a powerful tool parents have to help their kids tap into those reserves of perseverance and self-reliance. But you only get that by pushing your kids past the point of comfort. You only get that by teaching them humility and hard work.

TEACH YOUR KIDS TO SUFFER WELL

Jensen Huang, the CEO and founder of Nvidia, a leading tech corporation, recently spoke to students at Stanford University. While guest speakers are a regular feature at universities, Huang's comments to students made his speech quite memorable. "I wish you ample doses of pain and suffering," Huang told students. "Greatness is not intelligence. Greatness comes from character. And character isn't formed out of smart people, it's formed out of people who have suffered. Unfortunately, resilience matters in success. I don't know how to teach it to you except for I hope suffering happens to you."

Huang's message was one of unflinching truth. Unconventional compared to usual boilerplate speeches of working hard or staying positive, Huang emphasized that getting a top-rated education or the best internships are not predictors of success. Instead, he knows and has seen firsthand that resilience, grit, and determination make all the difference. These are what he looks for in job applicants; people with these traits lead to innovation and success.

Now, I'm not saying we must make our children unduly suffer, or become Navy SEALS, or never watch T.V. again. What I'm talking about is instilling a blue-collar mindset, a blue-collar soul into your kids. A soul of humility, of grit, of a tireless work ethic.

Parents have the absolute moral duty of teaching their kids to suffer well. That's not an idea, it's a habit. It's a disposition that's developed over time. So, parents ask yourself: when faced with suffering, can your kids tap into the extra reserves or not?

THE CODDLING CRISIS: A HISTORICAL PERSPECTIVE

To understand where we are, we need to look at where we've been. Post-World War II America saw a shift toward a more nurturing, child-centered approach to parenting. Dr. Benjamin Spock's 1946 book *The Common Sense Book of Baby and Child Care* encouraged parents to be more affectionate and responsive to their children's needs. While there are some, *some*, positive aspects to this emphasis, and while there were some, *some*, negative aspects to the pre-war authoritarian parenting, the net result is that we are in a mess today.

Fast forward to the 1980s and 1990s. Here we see the rise of the "helicopter parent." This term, coined by Dr. Haim Ginott, and popularized by Foster Cline and Jim Fay, described parents who hover over their children, ready to swoop in and solve any problem. The intentions were good—protect our kids, ensure their success—but the results? A generation of young adults who struggle with basic life skills and crumble at the first sign of adversity.

This reminds me of a funny incident years ago. We had friends over who had a two-year-old. We had a two-year-old son as well (we've had a two-year-old for over twenty years straight now). My son came up and asked Ashley,

"Can I have a yogurt?" "Sure," she said, and then continued talking to our visitors. My son pulled a bar stool across the kitchen floor to the fridge, climbed up, opened the fridge, pulled out a yogurt cup, closed the door, climbed down, pulled off the top of the yogurt cup, threw the lid in the trash can, then

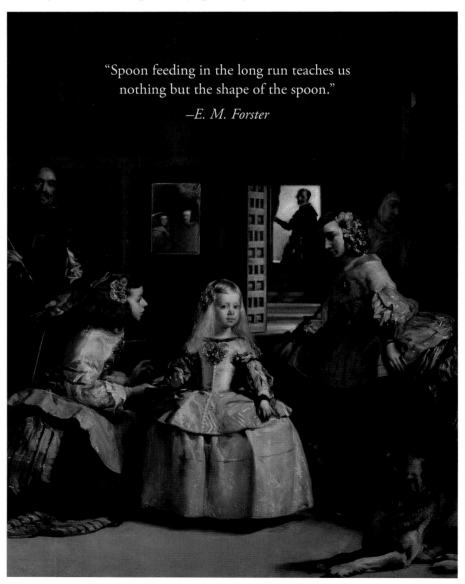

"Spoon feeding in the long run teaches us
nothing but the shape of the spoon."

—E. M. Forster

pulled the bar stool across the floor again to the silverware drawer with one hand (holding the yogurt in the other), climbed up, opened the drawer, took out a spoon, put the spoon in the yogurt, closed the drawer, climbed down, pulled the stool back to the bar, climbed up the stool, sat at the bar, and ate his yogurt. Our friends thought my kid was a genius. They were flabbergasted. About halfway through the event they were gawking at the kid in amazement. They explained their kid couldn't do anything for himself.

I asked a weird question. "If you dropped dead in your house, leaving your two-year-old to fend for himself for a few days, would he starve to death or figure out how to get stuff out of the fridge, or how to open a banana, or how to get bread off the top shelf?"

"I guess he'd figure it out," my friend said.

"Exactly," I said. "The only difference between your kid and ours is that we force our kid to do stuff for himself. Given that he has a ton of other kids in the family and mom is often busy with a newborn, he often does stuff for himself just for expediency. But so long as you're pampering your kid, he's going to keep crapping his pants."

Admittedly, this might be a weird way of getting the point across, but I think it worked.

Folks, we also know moms who have groceries delivered to their college kids dorm rooms. I totally get that mom wants to take care of her little baby…but stop! This is delaying a very important part of human maturation. Humans for all of time have had to leave the cave and go hunt down food. Your spoiled little twenty-year-old baby doesn't even have to take a spear with him when he goes to the local Publix and sorts through the sushi selection and buys it with your ApplePay. For the love of all that is good, stop ordering his groceries. "But he doesn't have a car?" Well then, make him eat in the cafeteria. Or make him take the subway. Or an Uber. Or . . . now imagine them doing what you and I had to do in college . . . sucking up to an upper classman so he'd give you a ride to the store! That's right, even social skills of corroborating with others is being stifled by everyone living like an English Aristocrat with servants bringing food to them.

If you don't want your kid to starve to death one day, stop sending them food!

CHECK YOUR PRIVILEGE AT THE DOOR

Let's get real. If you're reading this, chances are you've got it pretty good. But that comfort you've worked so hard for? It's your child's kryptonite. A 2023 Harvard study found that nearly 1 in 3 young Americans latch onto their parent's employer, earning 17% more because of it. Sounds great, right? Wrong. This privilege is creating a generation of kids who can't handle adversity. Instead of forging their connection and blazing their own trails, these kids choose the path of least resistance. While it might give them a job in the short term, they become yet another helpless cog in the machine of comfort.

I was a child of great privilege. We lived in an upscale, white-collar neighborhood. There wasn't much opportunity to work with your hands or work with the land. And we really didn't do many chores. Most of that work was hired out. My parents, thank God, instilled so many wonderful principles in us, particularly the Faith, and they taught us hard work in other ways. But I'm not sure I ever fixed anything or built anything or cleaned anything until I was married.

When I got married, I began to see these activities as ends in themselves. If cutting the grass was just a means to the end of having a nice lawn, then once I had money there was zero reason to cut grass. But what if cutting grass was an end in itself? What if cutting wood and building a work bench or garden boxes was an end in itself? I wanted to learn a few things, and I did. And as time went on, I found that projects were extremely rewarding, particularly when done with the children. Mending a fence with your son is a marvelous event. And I've done just that.

Truth be known, I'm actually terrible at these things, but I've tried and gotten better. And my kids are better than me. I could easily afford a lawn service, but given that I have multiple teenagers, why would I deprive them of the great opportunity to build this little skill set, to encounter a sputtering small engine, to have to change oil and gas, or go with me to change the blades, and the pure joy of riding around and cutting grass. We'll talk more about rural life later on in this book. But suffice it to say, if you have privilege, check it at the door and go do stuff.

In short, parents, your overprotectiveness is crippling your children. A 2012 study published in the *Journal of Anxiety Disorders* found that overprotected children are more prone to worry and anxiety.[1] When parents constantly hover over their kid's shoulder, it instills the false worry in the kid that he's doing something wrong or that he's not capable or smart enough to be self-reliant. You're not just coddling them; you're setting them up for a lifetime of mental health issues. A 2022 study in *Frontiers in Psychology* linked overprotective parenting to higher occurrences of anxiety and depression in adult life.[2] Is that what you want for your kids?

SWEAT EQUITY: THE CURRENCY OF CHARACTER

Here's a wake-up call: chores aren't just about a clean house; they're about building character. A 20-year study published in the *Journal of Developmental and Behavioral Pediatrics* found that the best predictor of young adults' success in their mid-20s was whether they participated in household tasks at age 3 or 4.[3] The study found that when kids engage in activities that benefit the household and that require them to problem-solve or push themselves either mentally or physically, they develop a strong foundation of self-confidence and positive work-ethic. Yet, how many of us are robbing our kids of this crucial life lesson?

The American Academy of Child and Adolescent Psychiatry emphasizes that chores help children feel competent and responsible. They learn time management, organization, and the satisfaction of contributing to their family. But in our rush to ensure academic success, we're neglecting these fundamental life skills.

In my house, chores are a big deal. Our chore chart (*on the next page*) is like a heartbeat. Here, you can see how it works. Every night after dinner, I'm walking over to the chore chart and yelling (rather loudly) who has what chores. I expect them to get on it.

---

1 Susanne Knappe et al, Characterizing the association between parenting and adolescent social phobia, *Journal of Anxiety Disorders*, vol. 26, Issue 5, 2012, 608-616.

2 Vigdal, Julia Schønning, and Kolbjørn Kallesten Brønnick. "A Systematic Review of "Helicopter Parenting" and Its Relationship With Anxiety and Depression." *Frontiers in psychology* vol. 13. 25 May. 2022.

3 White, Elizabeth M et al. "Associations Between Household Chores and Childhood Self-Competency." *Journal of developmental and behavioral pediatrics: JDBP* vol. 40 (2019): 176-182.

Daily Chores

SUNDAY	MONDAY	TUESDAY	WEDNESDAY
Peter	Jude	David	Imelda
Jude	Peter	Imelda	David
Paul	Teresa	Jude A.M. Paul P.M.	Annie
Teresa	Paul	Annie	Luke/ Thomas
Imelda	David	Peter	Paul

Inside

THURSDAY	FRIDAY	SATURDAY	
Annie	Teresa	Paul	Dishes
Jude A.M. Paul P.M.	Paul	Teresa	Countertops
Imelda	Peter	Jude	Kitchen / Dining Room Floors
David	Jude	Peter	Rest of Downstairs
Jude	Luke/ Thomas	Imelda	Bonus Room Pick Up / Vacuum

The more teenagers we have (right now our 7th child is 14, but the kids graduate from the chore chart at 18) the more difficult it is to get them to do their chores on time. They are gone. They have tons of activities. So, we have to ride them pretty hard. If they are going out to basketball practice or to hang out with friends, they *need* to knock out as much of their chore as possible. And if no one finishes it off by the time they have returned home, they have to do it, no matter how late. Imagine if I just let teenagers off the hook. They'd become spoiled very quickly. They have to contribute to this family, lest they think they are white-collar kids.

My kids haven't a clue about our financial resources. Why? Because I want them to never expect a handout. My two oldest kids, both married with a child, just purchased their own homes. It was amazing. Neither expected their mother and me to help in any way with a down payment. So, when we told them how we would like to contribute to their first home, they were totally surprised, extremely grateful, and both expressed hesitation to accept a financial gift. (It has been Ashley's and my long-term goal to help each kid purchase a home.) I was so proud of them. They ain't perfect, but they ain't spoiled—at all. We've raised them to expect little from others and a lot from themselves. And we are seeing the tremendous reward right before our eyes.

So don't be surprised that overprotective parenting is associated with low self-efficacy later in life. A 2014 study in the *Journal of Child and Family Studies* found that children of helicopter parents had lower scores on self-efficacy measures.[4] "Helicopter parenting can be particularly harmful during emerging adulthood when young adults are working toward developmental goals of self-reliance and autonomy," researchers found. "Whereas some parental protection of their children is a positive quality, helicopter parenting occurs in situations that do not warrant parental involvement. For example, a parent may contact their child's professor to dispute their child's low grade or contact a potential employer to negotiate their child's job offer and salary."

By constantly monitoring and protecting your children, you're sending a clear message: they're not capable of managing life by themselves. They're not

---

4 Kouros, Chrystyna D et al. "Helicopter Parenting, Autonomy Support, and College Students' Mental Health and Well-being." *Journal of child and family studies* vol. 26 (2017): 939-949.

capable of taking care of themselves, or saving money, or one day buying a home early in their marriage. Is that really the legacy you want to leave?

And by the way, don't you just love it when Ivy League-type studies prove to you what your common sense already knew? I cite many studies in this little book to show that even the crazy "experts" are seeing what you and I already know.

COMFORT IS THE ENEMY: EMBRACE THE STRUGGLE

Listen up, because this is crucial: your love for your children shouldn't be measured by how comfortable you make their lives but by how well you prepare them for life's challenges. What are your kids learning?

Dr. Angela Duckworth, author of *Grit: The Power of Passion and Perseverance*, argues that grit—a combination of passion and perseverance—is a better predictor of success than IQ or talent.[5]

When I first read this book, I looked throughout our sales organization and saw that the great salespeople came from a diverse background: some had been in sales for decades, some were from the ministry, some were farmers, including a former Amish fellow. Their personalities were likewise diverse: some were extraverted, others introverted; some were detail oriented, some were oblivious to details. But what was the one thing that all of them had in common? Grit. The good ones all had a perseverance, a resilience, a courage. Grit is the perfect word. Just like my sales organization, your family is made up of radically different attributes. If you have two kids, you like tell people they are opposites. Even with sixteen, I like to say they are all opposites (and then people have to think about that for a second). But what you, dear parent, can instill in your child's soul, no matter their God-given attributes, is grit. Grit: what a lovely word precisely because it is a little dirty. Such is life. And such can your child be, but only if you allow your kid to flex that muscle through discomfort and struggle.

Haven't we all seen this in our friends, families, and colleagues? Is the smartest person really the most successful? In fact, I have said many times as an employer that the best thing that could happen to that guy or gal is to lose

---

5 Duckworth, Angela, *Grit: The Power of Passion and Perseverance* (New York: Scribner, 2016) 15-26.

about 10 IQ points. Academic aptitude inflates people's ego faster than anything. They become elite in their minds. They move their soul into an Ivory Tower above everyone else. The one industry where this doesn't seem to hurt people too much is academics. But in the rest of the world, arrogance comes back around to bite you.

We spend way too much time as a nation praising our kids' academic achievements. Do me a favor: if you have a bumper sticker that says, "My kid is an Honor Roll student as Jefferson Middle School" please, I beg you, for the love of all that is good, rip the damn thing off. And then explain to your kid that their academics, while important, is not near the most important thing to be proud of. Would you have a bumper sticker that says, "My kid prays every morning before going to Jefferson Middle School" or "My kid sticks up for the fat kids at Jefferson Middle School" or "My kid is kind to nerds at Jefferson Middle School" or "My kid doesn't watch porn like the other kids as Jefferson Middle School." I don't think so. But each of these is 10X more important than his stupid GPA. Don't communicate the wrong message, mom and dad. If you advertise what you are proud of to every person on the road, it's going to reprioritize what your kid sees as important.

Speaking of middle school, your overprotectiveness can also make your children prime targets for bullying. A 2013 study published by BBC News found that overprotected children are more likely to experience bullying in school.[6] Why? Because you've infantilized them, denying them the chance to develop conflict management and self-defense skills. Is this how you protect them?

"Children need support but some parents try to buffer their children from all negative experiences," said Professor Dieter Wolke, lead researcher in the study. "In the process, they prevent their children from learning ways of dealing with bullies and make them more vulnerable."

He added: "It is as if children need to have some distress so that they know how to deal with conflict. If the parents all the time do it for them then the children don't have any coping strategies and are more likely targets."

---

6 Richardson, H., "Overprotected children 'more likely to be bullied.'" BBC News, April 26, 2013. https://www.bbc.com/news/education-22294974

When you as parents jump in to solve every problem, coddle every tantrum, fold to every demand, you take the vital moments of learning invaluable skills right out from under them. While these moments in raising children can be hard—especially with younger children—you must remember that giving into demands or coddling poor behavior only make it harder. Your job is to instill responsibility and self-efficacy. Your job is to raise self-assured kids who have grit and integrity. This can only happen if you lead by example and give your children the opportunity to learn these skills.

YOUR NEW PARENTING MANTRA: "FIGURE IT OUT"

Parents, it's time for a new approach. Instead of jumping in to solve every problem for your kids, start saying, "Figure it out." It's not cruel; it's an act of love. You're building problem-solving skills that will serve them for life.

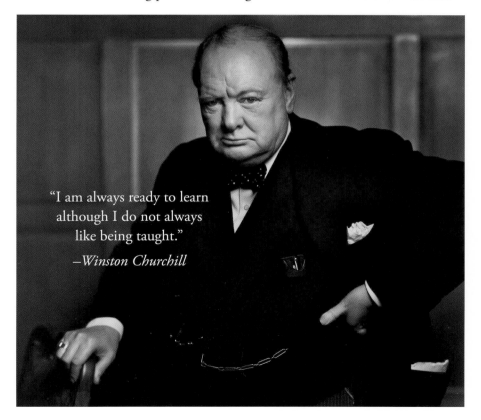

"I am always ready to learn although I do not always like being taught."
—*Winston Churchill*

Dr. Madeline Levine, psychologist and author of *The Price of Privilege*, warns that when parents routinely step in to prevent their children from failing, they interfere with the child's development of self-efficacy—the belief in one's ability to handle life's challenges.[7]

"Intrusion and support are two fundamentally different processes: support is about the needs of the child, intrusion is about the needs of the parent," Levine writes. "Children need work experiences to develop a sense that success is a function of their own efforts….We all want our children to put their best foot forward. But in childhood and adolescence, sometimes the best foot is the one that is stumbled on, providing an opportunity for the child to learn how to regain balance, and right himself."

Studies show that children of overprotective parents often engage in risk-taking behaviors later in life. They either become excessively fearful and timid, or wildly rebellious. Why? I think it's because they did not experience risk and reward enough early in life. It's as if that part of the brain doesn't work yet. Kids need to fail. Kids need to feel the pain of failure. It is the pain of failure that helps them make better risk assessments later in life.

I remember one day my sixteen-year-old son had a front headlight go out. He wanted to take it to the dealership. I told him not a chance. He had two options: 1) go to YouTube and figure it out, or 2) go to O'Reilly Auto Parts, talk to someone there, and figure out how to do this. It took him a few hours, but he did it. Sounds small. It is. Yet it is atomic. Even in a little lesson like this, it starts small but a huge atomic habit is built in which he learned to problem solve himself, to not be afraid of getting his hands dirty and stumbling through a learning process.

THE RIPPLE EFFECT: HOW YOUR PARENTING SHAPES SOCIETY

Parents, the stakes are higher than you might realize. We're not just raising kids; we're shaping the next generation of adults who will lead our communities, run our businesses, and govern our nation. The consequences of overprotective parenting extend far beyond your family.

---

7 Levine, Madeline, *The Price of Privilege* (New York: Harper, 2006).

A 2023 study by Gallup found that only 36% of U.S. employees are engaged in their work in 2020 and has dropped even lower since.[8] Could this be a result of a generation raised to expect constant guidance and praise, now struggling in workplaces that demand initiative and resilience? Could it be that they go from mommy and daddy telling them how special they are to the boss telling them how inadequate their work product is? As a nation, we are creating an economy of white-collar wimps.

Remember, every time you rescue your child from a challenge, you're stealing an opportunity for growth. Every time you solve a problem for them, you're robbing them of the chance to develop critical thinking skills. Every time you shield them from discomfort, you're weakening their ability to cope with life's inevitable hardships.

The choice is yours, parents. Will you continue to handicap your children with overprotection, or will you have the courage to step back and let them grow? The future of your children—and our society—depends on your answer. We need blue-collar mindsets more than we need technological revolution. We don't need faster microchips. We need workers who don't need safe places to scream and cry.

It's time to ditch the white-collar mindset and embrace the grit, resilience, and work ethic that will truly set our children up for success. It won't be easy, but then again, nothing worth doing ever is. Your kids are counting on you. Let's get to work.

---

8 Harter, B. J., "U.S. Employee Engagement Needs a Rebound in 2023". Gallup.com, January 25, 2023.

YOU MUST INSTILL

THE HABIT OF

HARD WORK

IN YOUR CHILD

CHAPTER

2

CHORES: YOUR SECRET WEAPON FOR SUCCESS

When it comes to parenting, one of the most powerful tools you have at your disposal is often overlooked: chores. Yes, chores. They're not just about keeping the house clean; they're about building character, instilling work ethic, and preparing your children for the real world. It's time to wake up and realize that assigning chores is one of the best gifts you can give your kids.

My fifteen-year-old Paul and seventeen-year-old Jude both work at the local bagel shop. Paul needed a drive this morning at 6:30 a.m. because Jude is sick with strep throat. When I dropped Paul off, I ordered a sandwich for breakfast. The owner came out, shook my hand and said, "The good thing about Jude is when he says he's sick, I know he must be really sick. That kid works hard and would never fake it." That happened three hours ago, no joke. It happens all the time with my kids. It makes me proud. The entire environment Ashley and I have constructed produces strong work ethics in our kids. But the short cut way we encouraged such work ethic is that they had a ton of chores growing up.[1]

Now, Jude is pretty darn sick. He's excused from his chores. This is a great opportunity for other kids to practice generosity, charity, and hard work. Last night, by way of example, Jude had floors (which means sweeping the kitchen and dining room). Imelda, twelve-years-old, was asked to take on Jude's chores. I saw Imelda's somewhat curmudgeon face. I asked what the problem was. She explained that the night before she had to fill-in for Annie (age nine) because she was sick. So, Imelda had double chores two nights in a row. Now, parents, listen up. I could have expressed my sympathy for her; I could have struck a deal with her that Jude and Annie will do her chores next week. But no. I asked her why it was important to be thankful for her ability to fill-in for her siblings. I asked her why God would have organized the entire universe in such a way that Annie would be sick yesterday and Jude would be sick today, knowing that Imelda Rose Gallagher would get double chores two days in a row. Why? Why should Imelda be grateful for this situation? She thought for a moment (while continuing to sweep) and said, "I guess because it teaches me charity." Bingo!

Not only was this an opportunity for Imelda to get a little grittier, it was an opportunity for her to practice virtue. And God planned it that way. It's my job to make sure she participates and recognizes the divine reality at play. One day soon, Imelda's first boss at the bagel shop or the grocery store will shake my hand and say, "She works so hard."

My kids aren't perfect, but they aren't wimps. Chores, perhaps more than anything else, fosters a blue-collar soul, which is so desperately needed in our white-collar world.

---

1 There is one critical distinction to add. Ashley and I are very aware that our children have free-will and have made the decision as teenagers to work hard, to be responsible and reliable. Sure, we have to take a little credit for the household they grew up in. But we don't want credit for their young adult successes. It belongs to them. They could easily have rejected what we have taught them and go down a radically different path. So, while we get a little credit, the lion's share belongs to them.

"The only place success comes before work is in the dictionary."

—Vince Lombardi

THE CHORE CONNECTION: RESEARCH AND RESULTS

Let's start with some hard facts. A 2019 study published in the *Journal of Developmental and Behavioral Pediatrics* found that children who engage in household chores are more likely to develop essential life skills and exhibit higher levels of success in adulthood. The researchers tracked a group of children over 20 years and discovered that those who participated in regular chores as kids were more likely to earn higher incomes and report greater job satisfaction.[2]

In another study conducted by the University of Minnesota, researchers found that children who did chores at age three or four were better prepared for adulthood than those who did not.[3] The study highlighted that these children demonstrated better self-regulation, social skills, and a sense of responsibility by their mid-20s.

Now, why do chores have such a significant impact? It boils down to the development of critical life skills. When children take on responsibilities at home, they learn time management, organization, and the satisfaction that comes from completing a task. They also learn that effort leads to results—a lesson that will serve them well throughout their lives.

But I actually think the study is missing an important reason for the correlation. Aristotle was the master at explaining how virtue is developed. Virtue is a habit, a habit of finding the mean between two extremes. Chores help kids build the right habits. It is a muscle they flex for years and years at home, and this follows them into their careers.

---

2 White, Elizabeth M et al. "Associations Between Household Chores and Childhood Self-Competency." *Journal of developmental and behavioral pediatrics: JDBP* vol. 40,3 (2019): 176-182.

3 Wallace, Jennifer, "Why children need chores." Wall Street Journal, April 13, 2013.

What habits are being formed?

- Willingness and ability to do the same mundane thing every day
- Willingness and ability to follow rules and a system
- Recognition that work comes first, then play
- Acceptance of being a team player in an environment much bigger than you
- Willingness and ability to wake up early to do farm chores
- Willingness and ability to stay up late and finish household chores

This list goes on and on.

When I see my teenager sweeping the floor or scrubbing a toilet with a sour look on his face, I smack him in the back and say, "You're building virtue! Isn't that exciting!" I know it is annoying, and I will always just get a depressed look back, but sometimes with a little smile creeping through the grimace. But this funny little way of doing it does, in fact, remind them that this is about more than having a clean home.

"I'M BORED": MUSIC TO A PARENT'S EARS

As parents, we often loath hearing our kids utter those dreaded words: "I'm bored." But what if I told you that boredom is an opportunity? A 2014 study by the University of Colorado at Boulder published in *Frontiers of Psychological f* found that unstructured time allows children to develop creativity and problem-solving skills.[4] When kids are bored, they're forced to think critically about how to entertain themselves.

"The more time that children spent in less-structured activities, the better their self-directed executive functioning," researchers reported. "The opposite was true of structured activities, which predicted poorer self-directed executive functioning."

Instead of rushing to fill their time with screens or structured activities, embrace boredom as a chance for growth. Children need such time to develop executive functions and build decision-making tools in their brains. For

---

4 Barker JE, Semenov AD, Michaelson L, Provan LS, Snyder HR and Munakata Y (2014) "Less-structured time in children's daily lives predicts self-directed executive functioning." Front. Psychol. 5:593. doi: 10.3389/fpsyg.2014.00593

example, when kids play "make-believe", they practice engaging self-directed forms of executive function by developing and maintaining their own goals to guide their behavior, the study shows. When your child complains about being bored, encourage them to find something productive to do, encourage them to use their imaginations and engage their minds. Only then do creative juices start to flow.

During the Covid shut down, my kids were getting pretty bored at home. So they decided to build a rather substantial mountain bike trail in the woods behind our house. They were out there for hours and hours each day. It was really impressive. They made jumps, cut down little trees, built little bridges across ditches. It was awesome. Boredom was the mother of this invention.

The glorious things kids can do with their free time is amazing. Little kids should be building forts. It burns energy outside in nature, but more importantly they play the role of architect. They envision a project. They cut and shape branches. They make defenses against enemies attacking through the woods. Their imagination runs wild. They watch their plan take shape. They watch their plans fail. They learn the realities of physics and gravity and other laws of nature beyond their control. Forts are glorious. Get your kids outside. Maybe you help them get started, but don't do everything. It ain't your fort; it's theirs.

What about older kids? Well, with YouTube, any kid can learn any instrument. When there is down time at my house (and there isn't a ton of it), you'll find two of my kids on YouTube learning new guitar songs. Paul can play seemingly every classic rock song I know on electric and my little Imelda loves playing the blues (which is kind of funny seeing this cute little girl playing the blues). And my wee-little kids (seven years old and down) learn to draw on this particular YouTube channel for kids. Everyone is filled with activities all the time. They use technology as a tool, not a pacifier, and motivate themselves to learn new skills.

In short, only boring people get bored. Don't let your kid become a boring person.

AGE-APPROPRIATE TASKS: FROM TODDLERS TO TEENS

One common misconception is that chores are only for older children. In reality, children as young as two can participate in age-appropriate tasks.

Here are some examples of age-appropriate chores:

- **Ages 2-4**: Simple tasks like putting away toys or wiping spills.
- **Ages 5-7**: Helping set the table, sorting laundry by color, or dusting low furniture.
- **Ages 8-10**: Making their beds, feeding pets, doing dishes, or vacuuming.
- **Ages 11-13**: Doing laundry, yard work, cleaning bathrooms, or helping with meal prep.
- **Ages 14+**: Managing their own schedules, cooking meals independently, or taking on larger household projects.

By gradually increasing responsibilities as they grow older, you empower your children with essential life skills while also teaching them accountability. Through chores, they learn task-oriented accomplishment and actively take part in the household and family system. They develop a certain pride of their work and effort, and this in turn helps them develop responsible stewardship for their home, possessions, and relationships.

Dr. Carol Dweck, renowned psychologist and author of *Mindset: The New Psychology of Success*, warns that praising children for their intelligence or talent, rather than their effort, can lead to a fixed mindset.[5] These kids become afraid of challenges, fearing failure will prove they're not as smart or talented as their parents believe. As your children take on real tasks and contribute to household goals and functions, they will see the fruits of their labors. They become empowered by being useful in real, practical ways, learning skills at the same time. Such skills and responsibility provide a strong footing for success in life.

WHEN TO STEP IN (SPOILER: ALMOST NEVER)

A man once told his son to go outside and move a great big stone from one side of the yard to another. The son first tried to push it. The stone wouldn't

---

5 Dweck, Carol S., *Mindset: The New Psychology of Success* (New York: Ballentine, 2007).

budge. Then he tied ropes around it and tried to pull it. No luck. Then he got a big stick and tried to use it like a lever to roll the stone. Nothing.

After giving it a valiant effort for more than an hour, the boy came in and said to his dad, "I can't do it. I've tried everything." The dad replied, "Son, I'm really proud of your great effort, your ingenuity, your determination. But you didn't try everything." "Yes, I did. I can't think of any other way to do it." "Well, son," the dad said, "you didn't try everything. You didn't try, after failing over and over again, to ask me for my help."

I love this story. It shows that parents must expect their kids, demand of their kids, to try and try and try again. Let your kids push their ingenuity, their creativity, their arms, legs, and backs. Let them put everything they have into it. But then, when they have reached their limit, mom and dad must be there to help, to comfort, to teach, to guide, and yes, to lift even the heaviest stones in the child's life. I will die for any of my kids without hesitation. I'm ready. Right now. I'm ready to be a martyr for them. But first, they need to push themselves to the limit so that one day they too will have the capacity to die for their own children.

As parents, it's tempting to step in when we see our children struggling— whether it's making their bed or washing dishes or switching out a headlight in their first car. But resist that urge! Guide them, give them little tips, like when I told my son to learn from YouTube or from O'Reilly Auto Parts on how to switch out the headlight. But don't do it for them.

When your children are allowed to complete tasks independently they develop greater self-efficacy—the belief in their ability to succeed. Whether it's your four-year-old trying to build Legos or your seventeen-year-old trying to fill out college applications, your kid needs to come face-to-face with a difficult task and find the grit to push through it. This is how they learn perseverance. But if mom and dad are right there to swoop in and take over, they only learn to give up. When you intervene too quickly or take over a task entirely, you send the message that your child isn't capable of handling it on their own. Instead of rescuing them from frustration, encourage them to persevere through challenges. Let them figure out how to wash dishes without breaking anything or how to fold laundry without your guidance.

FAMILY PROJECTS: BUILDING SKILLS AND BONDS

Chores don't have to be solitary tasks; they can also be opportunities for family bonding. Engaging in family projects—like gardening or home improvement—allows everyone to contribute while learning new skills together.

Research shows that families who work together on projects report stronger relationships and improved communication skills among family members.

In the Gallagher family, we have wonderful memories of building projects. My older kids still reminisce about the tree house I built with them. It was awesome. It even had a little front porch. Just recently, we looked on Zillow at the old house and saw pictures of the backyard. The kids and I were sad to see that finally the tree house was taken down 15 years later. But see that! My kids remember the whole process vividly. (And my wife and I vividly remember my battles with the stupid HOA Bolsheviks because I never got "permission" to build it.)

THE ALLOWANCE TRAP: WORK ISN'T ALWAYS ABOUT MONEY

Many parents struggle with whether or not to tie allowances to chores. While it may seem logical to pay kids for completing tasks around the house, research suggests this approach can backfire by promoting entitlement rather than responsibility.

A study conducted by researchers at the University of California found that when children receive money for doing household chores, they often view these tasks as optional rather than necessary contributions to family life.[6] Instead of focusing solely on financial rewards for chores, emphasize the intrinsic value of contributing as part of a family unit.

Here's a little confession. I remember when I was in high school. My dad had just started a new business with his partner that included a substantial pick and pack operation. It is now called catholiccompany.com, probably the most successful Catholic online retailer in the world. It was near Christmas, and the orders had piled up. He asked me if I would go to the warehouse on

---

6 Klein, W., Graesch, A. P., & Izquierdo, C. (2009b). Children and Chores: A Mixed-Methods Study of Children's Household Work in Los Angeles Families. *Anthropology of Work Review*, 30(3), 98–109.

Saturday and help pick and pack. To my utmost shame, I remember saying to him, "Yes, I can do that, but can I get better pay than you gave me last time? I can make more than that bagging groceries." A look of anger but also disappointment shot over his face. He said, "Sure, son. I'll pay anything you want. Does that make you feel better?" Oh man. I felt like dirt. I think that arrogance, that white-collar mindset of mine, was partially born from lacking some blue-collar lifestyle. I had very few chores. And I got an allowance for breathing. I was lazy and I was bit spoiled, though raised with great principles and faith and common sense.

I don't think many of my kids would say to me what I had said to my dad. If they did, I'd be one pissed off dad. In fact, I have enlisted them to work in my own warehouse (I also had a pick and pack operation for a number of years). And as my kids got older, they worked in the warehouse whenever we needed the help. I can't recall ever being asked for more money. In fact, I recall my oldest son trying to insist that he work for free because, "Dad needs the help." He's still that way. He's twenty-three years old and *wants* to help his mother and me in any way. Admittedly, I can think of one or two of my kids who have the propensity to take the easy way out and may well complain if I asked them for a Saturday of work.

I believe that the prevailing spirit of hard work in my family is due to my kids having a ton of chores, and my own arrogant, obnoxious, humiliating, self-centered, self-absorbed comment to my dad all those years ago was due to the fact that a) I'm a jerk, and b) I had very few chores. I pray that over time I have become a blue-collar man so that I could be better at raising blue-collar kids. This takes effort and persistence. And the more money one makes, the greater the temptation to "outsource" everything, freeing oneself from getting dirty. The temptation for busy executives is that they need rest and should not be bothered with physical labor. In reality, hard work is a great way to purge the mind. All one must do is envision Ronald Regan famously chopping wood at his range when on vacation from the White House. He obviously didn't need to do that. But his soul craved the natural order. And it made him a little more equipped to walk back into the white-collar world and be his very best.

Recently, I literally knocked myself completely unconscious with a farm jack. I was jacking up my zero-turn lawn mower to fix a broken piece underneath. Well . . . I failed to click the farm jack all the way down. So, the weight of the mower caused the handle of the jack to fly back up, hitting me in the jaw. My fifteen-year-old Paul saw the whole thing. I don't remember much. About a minute later, I came to. My wife was by my side all of a sudden, and she loaded me in the car and took me to the ER. Big deal. I got my bell rung. I'm fortunate it didn't hit my throat.

You see, I'm terrible at this stuff. One might say I have no business using any farm equipment. I can easily pay a guy to handle this stuff. But I feel it is important for my son to be out there with me, trying to fix the darn lawn mower (which I did a week later). It is quite embarrassing how challenged I am in these areas, but it's good for my soul and it's good for my kids to see me trying, even if I do have a permanent lump on my jaw line now.

CONCLUSION: CHORES AS LIFE LESSONS

Chores are not just mundane tasks; they are essential life lessons wrapped in everyday responsibilities. By assigning age-appropriate tasks and allowing your children the freedom (and challenge) of completing them independently, you're equipping them with valuable skills they'll carry into adulthood.

The research is clear: children who engage in household chores grow into responsible adults who excel personally and professionally. They learn resilience through struggle and satisfaction through hard work—qualities that will serve them well throughout life's challenges.

So embrace those chore charts! Celebrate every completed task! And remember that every time your child picks up a broom or folds laundry without being asked, they're not just helping out, they're building character.

As parents committed to raising strong individuals capable of facing life's challenges head-on, it's time we recognize the power of chores as our secret weapon for success.

LET YOUR

CHILDREN FAIL

SO THEY CAN

FIND THE GRIT

TO KEEP GOING

C H A P T E R

3

TOUGHENING
UP YOUR KIDS
(AND YOURSELF)

In today's world of bubble-wrapped childhoods and participation trophies, we're facing a crisis of resilience. Our kids are softer than ever, and it's time to face an uncomfortable truth: we, as parents, are largely to blame. But don't worry, it's not too late to turn things around. This chapter is about toughening up—not just your kids, but yourself too. Because let's face it, raising resilient children requires resilient parents.

HELICOPTER PARENTS, IT'S TIME TO LAND

As I mentioned in Chapter 1, the term "helicopter parent" was coined back in 1969 by Dr. Haim Ginott, but it's become increasingly relevant in recent decades. These are the parents who hover over their children, ready to swoop in at the first sign of difficulty. Sound familiar? If you're wincing, you're not alone.

A 2018 study published in the journal *Developmental Psychology* found that children with helicopter parents were more likely to struggle with emotional regulation and school engagement.[1]

"Our research showed that children with helicopter parents may be less able to deal with the challenging demands of growing up, especially with navigating the complex school environment," said Nicole B. Perry, PhD, from the University of Minnesota, and lead author of the study. "Children who cannot regulate their emotions and behavior effectively are more likely to act out in the classroom, to have a harder time making friends and to struggle in school."

But here's the kicker: a 2019 study from the University of Arizona found that over-parenting doesn't just affect kids—it's bad for parents too, fueling their own anxieties and harmful perfectionism mindset. Helicopter parents reported lower life satisfaction and less meaning in their lives.

"We started giving kids trophies at the end of the season just for being on the team, not because they actually achieved anything," said University of Arizona researcher Chris Segrin. "Fast-forward 35, 40 years and these people are now adults who have children who are entering into adulthood. They were raised in a culture of 'you're special, you're great, you're perfect,' and that fuels perfectionistic drives. 'If I really am special, if I really am great, then my kids better be special and great, too, or it means I'm not a good parent.'"[2]

In essence, this habit comes of a desire to control outcomes. You want your kids to be good people. You want to be a good person. So you try to overcompensate and play god. But the reality is, you're not. And more harm is being done to both you and your child when you try to micromanage and control every aspect of their lives.

So, for everyone's sake, it's time to step back.

I can't say that Ashley and I were ever helicopter parents. But of course we gave an extra dosage of attention and oversight to our older kids. The best example is with sports. My oldest was a serious baseball player: a switch-hitting

---

1 American Psychological Association. (2018, June 18). *Helicopter parenting may negatively affect children's emotional well-being, behavior* [Press release]. https://www.apa.org/news/press/releases/2018/06/helicopter-parenting

2 *Perfectionists May be More Prone to Helicopter Parenting, Study Finds* | University of Arizona News. (n.d.). https://news.arizona.edu/news/perfectionists-may-be-more-prone-helicopter-parenting-study-finds

catcher. And like many dads, I threw myself into Aiden's baseball career. We had a batting cage, got him personal training, he played for competitive teams, and he played multiple seasons in one year.

I remember thinking that I had to be at every game. And when he was younger, every practice! How foolish. Due to the size of our growing family, I was forced out of this mindset. Loving your kid doesn't mean always being there on the sidelines or hovering over his shoulder constantly. It means raising your kid in an environment conducive to virtue development.

LET THEM FALL: THE ART OF NATURAL CONSEQUENCES

One of the most powerful tools in a parent's arsenal is something counterintuitive: letting your kids fail. Natural consequences are the real-world results of a child's actions or decisions, and they're far more effective teachers than any lecture you could give.

Dr. Jessica Lahey, author of *The Gift of Failure*, argues that allowing children to experience failure is crucial for their development. She cites research showing that children who are protected from failure have higher rates of anxiety and lower resilience when faced with real-world challenges.

Research shows that children who are allowed to experience natural consequences show improved decision-making skills and higher levels of responsibility compared to those whose parents frequently intervened. If you tell your son to put his toys away before the puppy chews them, but he refuses, the puppy will chew them. He'll get upset, but next time you can bet he'll put them away. But if the parent steps in and cleans up for him, nothing is learned, and the lesson he must learn is put off again.

"Failure is simply the opportunity to begin
again, this time more intelligently."

–Henry Ford

Another baseball story comes to mind. I was a little league baseball coach for my third, fourth, and fifth kids. The last game of the season was over. And we are gathered together behind the dugout to congratulate each other on a fun season.

The day before I had to submit my selection of All-Star players from my team to the league. Well, what better time to celebrate these kids' achievement than with their teammates and the parents?

So, I asked three kids to step forward, but then the assistant coach ran up and pulled me aside, whispering, "You can't announce them as All-Stars!"

"Why the hell not?" I asked.

"Because it will make the other kids feel bad."

"Well," I said, "tough. That's life."

And then he said, "The parents of the other kids are going to kill you."

"Are you serious?" I asked in surprise.

"Conor, I'm dead serious. You will regret it."

And so, in my utter dismay, I returned to the crowd, and the three kids awkwardly standing in front of everyone, and I made up something about how these kids had good plays in the game we just had.

At the time, I was mad at the situation. Now, I'm mad at myself for caving in.

How absurd! Kids must learn that they aren't always number one. They must learn that others are better at things. They must learn that the dumbest thing anyone ever told them is that "You can do anything if you put your mind to it." Anyone with a brain knows this is stupid. Failure makes us strong. And by the way, not being number one is not the same thing as failure. Kids who don't make the All-Star team aren't failures. They just aren't the All-Stars.

A famous example of this is the Irish author James Joyce. Despite being one of the greatest and most influential writers in history, he never won a single award for his work, and many didn't sell well at all. Did this dimmish his ego or make his work meaningless? Absolutely not. He continued working hard and writing his best because that's who he was. He had grit and perseverance, and that lasts forever.

White-collar kids live in a sheltered world in which their ego is protected at all costs. A blue-collar culture, one closer to nature, one that is tied more to the earth, to the crafts, to physical labor, instills a sense of respect for winning and losing, for learning from mistakes. Ego is checked at the door. It instills a resilience that the white-collar coddling does not. Blue-collar kids know how to take a physical and psychological punch. And that's an important lesson in life.

In a blue-collar world, not everyone is an All-Star. In a white-collar world, everyone pretends that they are.

"THAT'S NOT FAIR!": THREE MAGIC WORDS FOR GROWTH

If you're a parent, you've heard it a thousand times: "That's not fair!" But instead of seeing this as a complaint to be quashed, view it as an opportunity for growth. Life isn't fair, and the sooner kids learn this, the better equipped they'll be to handle real-world challenges.

Dr. Kenneth Ginsburg, author of "Building Resilience in Children and Teens," emphasizes the importance of helping children develop a realistic view of the world. He argues that children who understand and can cope with unfairness are better prepared for life's inevitable disappointments.

"What does it do to children when they are raised in a culture, where, to be noticed, you have to be the very best? And to be destroyed, you need only be caught making a mistake," Dr. Ginsburg writes. "The most essential ingredient in raising resilient children is an adult who loves or accepts them unconditionally and holds them to high but reasonable expectations. High expectations are not about grades or performance. They're about integrity, generosity, empathy, and the traits our children need if they are to contribute to the world."

When raising blue-collar kids in a white-collar world, it's crucial to address the toxic obsession with fairness that permeates our society. This fixation on fairness is a poison for the soul, particularly detrimental to children's character development. When kids cry out, "It isn't fair!" parents must seize this as an opportunity to redirect their focus toward virtues within their control—compassion, charity, meekness, and humility.

Blue-collar folks inherently understand this reality. They face the stubborn mule that won't budge, the capricious weather that won't cooperate with their crops, and the machines that malfunction despite their best efforts.

These experiences teach them a valuable lesson: life isn't about controlling external circumstances but about mastering one's own attitude in the face of adversity.

"You have power over your mind, not outside events. Realize this, and you will find strength."

—*Marcus Aurelius*

In contrast, white-collar environments often foster the illusion of control. When the filet mignon isn't cooked to perfection or the valet service is slow, there's an expectation that the world should bend to one's will. This mindset is a disservice to children, setting them up for frustration and disappointment in a world that rarely conforms to their desires.

Parents must help their children understand that the question isn't whether something is fair, but whether they're bringing the proper attitude to the situation. When a child complains about unfairness, a parent might respond, "It's not a question of fairness. It's a question of your patience and willingness to endure a bit of injustice." This approach echoes Socrates's wisdom that it's better to suffer injustice than to commit it.

Moreover, there's a spiritual dimension to consider. Insisting on always getting the best deal or the fullness of one's due stands in stark contrast to Christ's willingness to suffer incredible injustice. Parents must find ways to communicate that refusing to suffer well is, in a sense, an injustice against Christ and His mystical body of disciples.

Much like the anecdote of my daughter Imelda complaining she had to take on her brothers' chores, there was an opportunity there for her to learn. And guess what, there will be many more. Life is replete with moments of injustice and unfairness. These are often entirely out of our control, but how we approach them, how we tap into our reserves of virtue and resilience and grit make all the difference. If you as a parent deprive your child of this early on, the world is going to hit them very hard later on, whether it's fair or not.

Moments like these must be seized and turned into opportunities for them to grow and learn.

Here are a few practical tips for parents when faced with this:

1. When hearing, "That's not fair," respond with, "How can you show patience in this situation?"
2. Encourage children to identify virtues they can practice when faced with perceived unfairness.
3. Share stories of historical figures or family members who thrived despite unfair circumstances.
4. Model graceful acceptance of life's inequities in your own behavior.
5. Discuss the concept of redemptive suffering in age-appropriate ways.

By shifting the focus from external fairness to internal virtue, parents can help their children develop the resilience and character needed to thrive in an imperfect world. This approach, rooted in blue-collar wisdom, prepares kids for the realities of life while nurturing their spiritual growth.

SCREEN TIME IS WEAK TIME: GET THEM OUTSIDE

White-collar kids are increasingly growing up immersed in screens, with studies showing children as young as four months old regularly engaging with digital media. This excessive screen time is having profound effects on their development. Research indicates that higher levels of screen use in young children is associated with lower cognitive abilities, decreased academic performance, and impaired language development. For preteens and teenagers, excessive screen time correlates with higher rates of anxiety, depression, lower quality of life, and poorer psychological well-being. In 2024, the average kid spends an average of 8+ hours on screens. The average time kids spend outside engaging in free play fell to an astonishing 4 minutes per day. And to top that, the average attention span of children aged 7-18 dropped to just 8 seconds—one second less than the attention span of a gold fish.

Sure, technology has its uses. But this is ridiculous. Here are the most recent statistics:

Kids aged **8-10** spend an average of **6+ hours per day** on screens. In a year, that's equal to **91.25 days spent looking at a screen**.

Kids aged **11-14** spend an average of **9+ hours per day** on screen, equaling **136.88 days in a year**.

Teens aged **15-18** spend **8+ hours per day** on a screen, equaling **121.67 days in a year**.

Children/young adults **aged 12-25** check their phones an average of **150 times per day**.

Average attention span in 2024 dropped to **8 seconds**. (A gold fish's attention span is 9 seconds.)

42% of millennials haven't gone more than **5 hours** without looking at **social media**.

In 2024, kids **ages 3-16** spent an average of **4 minutes playing outside**.

40% of 3-month-olds and **90% of 2-year-olds** are regularly watching programs on screens.

47% of kids receive a personal smart phone **by age 8**.

95% of children aged 10-18 have a smart phone.

Young children (**ages 1 to 8**) who spent more than 2 hours watching screens developed symptoms of **ASD (Autism Spectrum Disorder)** induced by screen time.

By 2023, a **66% increase of depression** occurred in teens who spend at least **2-3 hours a day** on social media (the average is **4.8 hours a day on social media** alone).

In 2024, kids **aged 8–17** spend an average of **1.5–2 hours per day playing video games** alone.

Dr. Peter Gray, research professor at Boston College, argues that the decline of free play in children's lives has contributed to the rise of anxiety, depression, and narcissism in young people. When we constantly structure and supervise our children's lives, we deny them the opportunity to develop critical social skills, emotional intelligence, and problem-solving abilities.

To cultivate a blue-collar soul in our children, it's crucial to significantly reduce screen time. Blue-collar work often involves hands-on skills, problem-solving in physical environments, and direct human interaction—experiences that excessive screen use can inhibit. By turning off screens, we allow children to engage more fully with the physical world around them, developing practical skills and resilience.

Staring blankly and passively into a screen not only diminishes brain activity and development, it is also linked to disrupting children's circadian rhythm and is even connected with Autism Spectrum Disorder. In fact, Dr. Jennifer McMahon, a clinical psychologist specializing in autism, suggests that parents conduct a four-week "electronic fast" if they are concerned with their child's behavior before bringing them in for assessment.[3]

The major factor is the child's engagement with the world around them. Sitting alone watching Sponge Bob for hours does nothing for them. But as soon as they get outside, their entire physiological makeup begins to change and get nutrients. From movement and fresh air to the sunlight itself, our bodies crave to be in the natural world. Kid's hands need to get dirty. They need to scrape their knees and get their pants muddy. They need to rake leaves, pull weeds, and build stick forts. They need to unplug and get outside again.

Limiting screen time encourages children to play imaginatively, engage in physical activities, and interact face-to-face with others. These activities foster creativity, improve social skills, and enhance cognitive development in ways that screens cannot replicate.

Implementing changes to screen time might be difficult at first, but the benefits will be noticed immediately. A few easy ways to start can be setting clear limits on screen time, create tech-free zones in the home, and have

---

3 Nunckley, V.L., MD. (2016, December 31). Children with autism are vulnerable to the negative effects of screen time. *Psychology Today*.

creative, hands-on activities ready that can replace screens. Encouraging out-door play, assigning age-appropriate chores, and engaging in family projects can help children develop the practical skills and work ethic associated with blue-collar values. By doing so, we can help our children develop the resilience, self-reliance, and hands-on problem-solving skills that will serve them well in any future career path. (See *WOF Digital Policy Builder*™ Tool on the next two pages.)

I've seen this principle in action with my own seven-year-old twins. Recently, they've been engrossed in building forts, and the transformation I've witnessed has been remarkable. They've been cutting down limbs and constructing these makeshift structures with an enthusiasm that no screen could ever match.

As I watch them work, I can see the wheels turning in their minds. They're not just playing; they're developing crucial skills. They're thinking like visionaries and architects, planning out their structures and figuring out how to bring their ideas to life. It's amazing to see how they're learning to translate their imagination into physical reality—a skill that's at the heart of so many blue-collar professions.

The physical aspect of their fort-building is just as important. As they cut limbs and assemble their creations, I can see the growing connection between their minds and hands. This kind of coordination is essential in blue-collar work, where you often need to apply physical skills based on mental calculations or plans. It's not something you can learn from a screen. While screens can get you started, just like a book or any learning tool, they can quickly become a detriment to learning skills. Developing essential skills requires hands on application and problem-solving in the moment.

But what's really struck me is how they handle setbacks. There have been times when their forts have collapsed, and I've watched with pride as they've picked themselves up, analyzed what went wrong, and started again. This cycle of failure, learning, and renewed effort is building a resilience that's at the core of a blue-collar soul. They're learning firsthand that success often comes through persistence and hard work, not instant gratification.

Watching my twins engage in this kind of play, I can see them developing the kind of practical intelligence and problem-solving skills that are

THE DIGITAL POLICY BUILDER™

Current State

WHAT WORKS: List any existing policies, formal or informal, that work well.	WHAT DOESN'T WORK: List any existing policies, formal or informal, that do not work well.

Future State

PURPOSE/OBJECTIVES: Craft a statement explaining why this is so important for the family and the individuals. Shape it in the form of parental love and affection. Also provide the goals or objectives of this policy.

When

Time of Day	Screen Time	Driving	Other
When can devices be in use? Is permission required? Is there a "docking" deadline?	List screen time limits per day, whether automated or manual.	Write down your expectations for driving safety and device use.	

Name: _____   Date: _____

1 of 2

THE DIGITAL POLICY BUILDER™

Who		Where	
Allowed Who are your children allowed to communicate with? Names or categories of people.	*Not Allowed* Who are they not allowed to communicate with? Names and categories.	*Allowed* Where can they use devices? In their rooms? Only in public spaces? Outside?	*Not Allowed* Where are devices not allowed? Be specific, such as "no phone zone."

What

Permitted content	Prohibited content
Permitted content List sites, games, shows, movies, or general content that is permitted.	*Prohibited content* List sites, games, shows, movies, or general content that is prohibited. Here, you need to be extremely specific.

Consequences of Violation

For willful violations, a punishment is recommended. This could be restriction from device, from social activities, increased chores, and so on.

Signatures

Name: _____   Date: _____

Well-Ordered Family

hallmarks of blue-collar wisdom. They're not just building forts—they're building character, resilience, and a blue-collar soul that will serve them well throughout their lives. It's a powerful reminder of why it's so important to turn off the screens and let our kids engage with the real world around them.

RURAL LIVING, RURAL MINDSET: EMBRACING THE GRIT

In our family, we've embraced rural living as a way to instill a blue-collar soul in our children. It's not just about living in the country; it's about adopting a mindset that values hard work, respects nature, and understands the cyclical rhythms of life.

Our garden has become a classroom for life lessons. I've watched my kids pull weeds from the gravel, their small hands learning the difference between unwanted growth and precious plants. They've experienced the joy of planting seeds, the patience of waiting for sprouts, and the satisfaction of harvesting what they've nurtured. There's nothing quite like seeing your child's face light up as they bite into a tomato they've grown themselves.

The yard work is endless, but that's the point. It teaches perseverance and the value of consistent effort. My teenage boys have become experts at cutting grass and blowing off the porch, understanding that maintaining our home is a never-ending task.

Our chickens have been a source of both joy and hard lessons. Every morning and evening, rain or shine, the kids are out there, tending to the coop. They've learned responsibility by collecting eggs for breakfast and compassion by putting warm cloths on the chickens at night. But nature isn't always kind. We've dealt with snakes eating eggs and raccoons killing chickens. My eleven-year-old, David, even learned to set traps for raccoons and possums when he was about nine years old. When we catch one, I have to execute it with my pistol. The kids watch, then dig a deep grave to dispose of the body. It's a harsh reality, but it teaches them about the circle of life and the sometimes difficult decisions we must make to protect what's ours.

Our Nigerian dwarf goats have been another source of learning. My girls clean out the stalls, learning that caring for animals isn't always glamorous. It's taught them commitment and the importance of following through on responsibilities.

I'm often on the tractor, tending to our gravel road. It's a constant battle against the elements, and the kids are always there, picking up displaced dirt and gravel. It's a tangible lesson in the ongoing effort required to maintain what we have.

We even tried our hand at beekeeping. My wife Ashley and I became certified beekeepers, but eventually, we had to give it up. It was a major chore, but it taught us and the kids about the complexity of nature and the importance of knowing when to persist and when to let go.

The point isn't that everyone must have a farm. The point is that kids benefit immensely from a rural lifestyle. Nature and hard work keep them grounded, teaching respect for the natural world. They never question whether you need a rooster and a hen to get more chickens. The difference between a stallion and a mare is obvious. The real world, the rural life, doesn't allow for nonsense ideologies.

"The wilderness: where the air is purer and the sky more open, and God is closer."

—Origen of Alexandria

There's a reason that rural communities tend to be more conservative. It's not that rural people are backward; they're tied to nature. They understand objective reality because they deal with it every day. The great John Senior, a professor at the University of Kansas, understood this. He took his ideologically infested 1960s students to his farm and had them build a door frame. You can't relativize a 90-degree angle. Nature doesn't care about your opinions; it demands respect and understanding.

For city dwellers looking to instill some of this rural mindset, there are options. Start a garden box or grow plants in your kitchen. Take weekend trips to the country. Visit petting zoos. Watch nature documentaries that show the real, sometimes harsh realities of the natural world. Let your kids see wild animals in their natural habitat, not just sanitized cartoon versions.

The goal is to give your children a taste of the natural world, to help them understand that there's an objective reality beyond human control. It grounds them, gives them perspective, and helps them develop a blue-collar soul that will serve them well, no matter where life takes them.

ORA ET LABORA: THE BENEDICTINE WAY OF LIFE

The Benedictine motto "Ora et Labora"—pray and work—encapsulates a lifestyle that naturally aligns with rural living. This ancient wisdom of monastic life, usually rooted in an agrarian lifestyle, offers profound lessons for modern families seeking to cultivate a blue-collar soul in their children. Since Saint Benedict (whom I discuss at fuller length in *The Architect*, another book in this series) started his first monastery in the 6th century, monks have worked the land, or at least earned their living by the sweat of their brow, and coupled this manual labor with prayer steadily ordered throughout the day.

Rural life and prayer are intimately connected. The rhythms of nature—sunrise, sunset, changing seasons—provide a natural framework for prayer and reflection. It's no coincidence that religious and even corporate retreats are often held in scenic, rural locations. The peace and beauty of the countryside allow for a deeper connection with the divine and oneself.

In our family, we've found echoes of the Benedictine way in our daily routines. Just as monks have a structured schedule for prayer and work, we've established our own rhythms. David's (our eleven-year-old) daily chicken chores mirror the monastic hours of Lauds and Vespers. Each morning and evening he's out there, rain or shine, tending to the flock. This consistency builds character and responsibility.

The routine of rural life toughens you up. There are always tasks that need doing, whether you feel like it or not. Milking cows, tending gardens, or repairing fences—these chores don't wait for convenience. They don't wait for you to feel like doing it. When a living animal is waiting for you, or a crop is going be destroyed by frost unless it is covered up, your feelings become rather irrelevant. Yet, there's a profound peace that comes from this structure. The early morning sun or the glow of moonlight becomes a comforting constant, marking the passage of time and the completion of honest work.

For families looking to incorporate this ethos, start small. Establish a vegetable garden, no matter how tiny. The act of planting, tending, and harvesting teaches patience, perseverance, and the rewards of hard work. Create a daily schedule that includes both work and moments of prayer. Even in urban settings, you can create a "rural" mindset by disconnecting from technology and reconnecting with natural rhythms.

This lifestyle produces a blue-collar soul by instilling values of hard work, humility, and respect for nature. Children raised in this way understand the dignity of labor and the satisfaction of a job well done. They develop resilience, problem-solving skills, and a deep-seated work ethic that will serve them well in any future endeavor.

By embracing elements of the Benedictine way, families can create a home environment that nurtures strength of character, practical skills, and a grounded perspective on life—the very essence of a blue-collar soul.

CONCLUSION: EMBRACING THE TOUGH LOVE REVOLUTION

Toughening up your kids—and yourself—isn't about being cruel or uncaring. It's about loving your children enough to prepare them for a world that won't always be kind or fair. It's about giving them the tools they need to navigate life's challenges with confidence and resilience. It's about empowering them to become the very people God is calling them to be.

Remember, every time you resist the urge to rescue your child from a difficult situation, you're giving them the gift of growth. Every time you encourage them to push through discomfort, you're helping them build mental and emotional strength. And every time you model resilience yourself, you're teaching them one of life's most valuable lessons.

Parenting isn't for the faint of heart. It requires courage, consistency, and a willingness to sometimes be the "bad guy." But the rewards—watching your children grow into capable, resilient adults—are worth every tough moment.

So, are you ready to join the tough love revolution? Your kids' future selves will thank you for it.

NATURE DEMANDS

DISCIPLINE

AND SO DO

YOUR CHILDREN

CHAPTER

4

DISCIPLINE: IT'S NOT A DIRTY WORD

In our twenty-four years of marriage, Ashley and I have watched too many kids abuse and beat the crap out of their parents. I have many imperfections as a dad, no doubt. But allowing my kids to bulldoze over me isn't one of them. We don't need stats to know that kids yell at mom and dad, swing at mom and dad, use nasty tones of voice with them, ignore them, and communicate disrespect in myriad ways. I'm amazed almost every time I'm out in public. I'm not amazed at the kid; I'm amazed at the parent letting the kid act that way.

"Johnny's just a strong-willed child," stupid parent says. We have literally, I kid you not, had people tell us we were so lucky for all of our children being born mild tempered and obedient. Wow.

Parents have been infected with a philosophy of permissive parenting. This is the style where parents think they're being nurturing and supportive. They set few rules or limits, allowing the kids a high level of freedom to make their own choices. This often makes the parent more like a friend than an authority figure, with minimal expectations and discipline for the children. In reality, this style "permits" the children to do whatever they want within reason and without much consequence. A main problem here (and there are a few) is that kids don't have much reason. They're still developing. They need their parents to show them the way, to lead them, not just stand by and let them do whatever they want.

The current generation of parents have been brainwashed into thinking that rules are restrictive, that corporal punishment is abuse, that forcing your kid to do what he does not want to do is stifling their creativity. We all see it: the parents in the restaurant trying to reason with a three-year-old about why they should not throw food; the parents in church handing their two-year-old a dozen different toys and a bag full of Cheerios to try keep them quiet. On occasion, I've heard middle school kids yell at mom or dad "Shut up!" when mom or dad began their half-ass attempt of discipline.[1]

Common sense parenting is no longer common. We have removed ourselves from nature to such an extent that we think theories will work with those who have not even reached the age of reason.

NATURE DEMANDS DISCIPLINE: LESSONS FROM THE RURAL LIFE

Blue-collar kids, especially those raised in rural settings, understand something that modern permissive parents often miss: nature must be worked with and sometimes manhandled, or disaster strikes. There's no room for ideology or theoretical debates when you're face-to-face with the raw realities of the natural world. If you don't tame a stallion, it becomes dangerous. If you don't establish yourself as the alpha with a dog, it will become unruly—or worse, violent. Nature demands discipline, and so do children.

---

1 There is a hilarious series of YouTube videos in which a teenager and Mom prank Dad. The prank is that they engage in a fake argument, and then the teenager yells as nastily as possible, "Shut up Mom!" The point of the prank is to see how Dad reacts. Every video has Dad oblivious to the argument, then he hears "Shut up Mom!", and he jumps out of his slumber like a bat out of hell, and rushes toward his teenager as if he is going to destroy him. Then Mom jumps in front and they try to explain the prank, pointing to the hidden camera. Admittedly, this is terrible. But I can't help but laugh hysterically at the zombie-like Dad who all of a sudden pops up and rushes his kid. I'm actually glad to see the Dads sort of freak out a little. The videos don't show the pansy Dads that just whimper out "Excuse me son, perhaps you should have a nicer tone of voice." We need real men putting their kids in their place. Note to my kids: NEVER do this prank on me.

On a farm, one learns firsthand that aggression isn't inherently bad—it's often necessary to maintain peace and order. When a raccoon starts killing chickens in the coop, you can't reason with it or hope it will stop because you've read a book on conflict resolution. You have to trap it, deal with it decisively, and protect what's yours. When a goat refuses to cooperate during milking or a garden becomes overrun with weeds, you can't sit back and hope for the best. You have to step in and take control.

This principle applies just as much to raising children as it does to managing nature. Discipline is about stepping in with authority when necessary—not out of anger or cruelty, but out of love and responsibility. A child left to their own devices without boundaries will become just as unruly as an untamed stallion or an untrained dog. Without discipline, chaos reigns.

"Seek freedom and become captive of your desires. Seek discipline and find your liberty."

—*Frank Herbert*

The problem with modern permissive parenting is that it's removed from these natural lessons. It relies on ideology and theories from parenting books written by people who've likely never had to pull weeds from a gravel path or fend off predators from their livestock. They talk about letting children "express themselves" without realizing that unchecked freedom leads to disorder. In nature—and in life—freedom without boundaries is destructive.

If we're removed from nature long enough, common sense itself becomes extinct. Rural life teaches us that discipline isn't just important—it's essential for survival. And what is parenting if not preparing your children to survive and thrive in the real world? Just as nature must be managed with firmness and care, so too must children be guided with discipline and love.

Parents need to reclaim this common-sense approach to discipline. It's not about being harsh; it's about being firm and consistent. Just as you wouldn't let a wild animal run loose in your home, you shouldn't let your child grow up without boundaries. Discipline is how we tame the wildness within them—not to break their spirit, but to shape it into something strong and beautiful.

RULES AREN'T SUGGESTIONS: SETTING NON-NEGOTIABLE CORE VALUES

Let's get one thing straight: rules aren't suggestions. They're the backbone of a well-functioning family and society. In blue-collar households, rules aren't just talked about, they're lived.

Start by identifying your family's core values (see *The Family Core Virtues Builder*™ Tool on the next page), or as the Well-Ordered Family management system calls them, core virtues. While in the business world or schools they talk about core values, I prefer to call them core virtues in the realm of family. The difference here is subtle but significant. While values tend to be subjective and vary from person to person, virtues have timeless, objective qualities. They are built into the very fabric of human nature.

So, as you're looking for those virtues you wish to see thrive in your family, begin by asking yourself: What matters most to you? Hard work? Honesty? Respect? Once you've nailed these down, establish non-negotiable rules that reflect these values. Maybe it's, "Everyone pitches in with chores" or "We always tell the truth, even when it's hard."

But here's the kicker: rules are useless if they're not communicated clearly and consistently. Sit your kids down and spell it out. No fancy language, no beating around the bush. "In this family, we show up on time. Period." Make sure everyone understands, from your toddler to your teenager.

And for the love of all that's holy, follow through! Nothing undermines your authority faster than empty threats. If you say there's a consequence for breaking a rule, you'd better be ready to enforce it. Every. Single. Time.

DIVINE ORDER: DISCIPLINE AS A PATH TO GODLINESS

The real tragedy of failing to establish and enforce rules in our homes goes far beyond immediate behavioral issues. It strikes at the very core of our children's spiritual development, potentially setting them up for a lifetime of struggle with the ultimate authority: Almighty God.

THE FAMILY CORE VIRTUES BUILDER™

Behaviors to Increase
What are the behaviors that bring joy and peace to your family?

How To Increase
Primary Obstacles: **Unique Opportunity:**

Behaviors to Decrease
What are the behaviors that induce tension in your family?

How To Decrease
Primary Obstacles:

Your Family's Core Virtues
Reflect on refining your lists of traits. Do you see commonalities? Can you create your own word or phrase that resonates with your family in a special way?

Name: Date:

Well-Ordered Family

God, in His infinite wisdom, has established divine laws governing not just the physical universe, but also our moral and spiritual lives. These aren't arbitrary rules, but guidelines designed for our wellbeing and flourishing. When children grow up in an environment where rules are mere suggestions and consequences are negotiable, how can we expect them to submit to the non-negotiable laws of God? By failing to discipline our children, we inadvertently teach them that authority is optional, boundaries are flexible, and consequences can be avoided—a mindset that is disastrous when applied to their relationship with God.

And once again, it's not about being harsh or cruel. Discipline is about stepping in with authority when necessary—not out of anger or cruelty, but out of love and responsibility. God gave the Israelites laws to teach them morality, set them apart from other pagan societies, and give them a path to holiness. Soldiers have strict discipline and rules to keep them and the man next to them alive. A mechanic shop has rules to ensure safety and that the work is done properly. Rules and discipline are not (and should never be) arbitrary ways of controlling others. They are methods to lead others to greatness.

Blue-collar jobs exemplify the importance of structure and discipline. In construction and manufacturing, strict safety protocols and operational guidelines aren't just arbitrary; they protect workers and ensure tasks are completed correctly and safely. This structured environment fosters a sense of discipline and accountability vital in blue-collar professions and spiritual life alike.

This adherence to rules partly explains why blue-collar societies tend to be more religious and God-fearing. The consistent structure in these jobs translates into a worldview valuing order, respect for authority, and understanding that actions have consequences—principles aligning closely with many religious teachings.

In contrast, the white-collar world often operates with less restriction, emphasizing autonomy and personal expression. This can lead to a fragmented sense of responsibility and a disconnect from traditional values, making it easier to drift from the moral compass that religion provides.

By raising kids in a blue-collar way—instilling discipline through clear rules, responsibilities, and consequences—we prepare them not just for career success, but for their eternal destination. They learn the value of hard work, respect for authority, and the importance of community—essential elements for a fulfilling life grounded in faith.

Remember, our goal isn't just to raise good citizens, but to nurture souls that understand, respect, and ultimately love the divine order established by our Creator. Discipline in the home isn't just about managing behavior—it's about preparing hearts to receive and follow God's perfect law, helping our children navigate life's challenges with resilience while keeping them aligned with their spiritual journey.

THE "NO" MUSCLE: STRENGTHENING YOUR RESOLVE

Parents, it's time to flex your "No" muscle. And to understand just how powerful "No" can be, let's take a lesson from Chris Voss, the former FBI hostage negotiator and author of *Never Split the Difference*.

Voss argues that "No" is actually stronger than "Yes." In negotiations, saying "No" gives people a sense of control and safety. It establishes boundaries and allows them to feel secure in their decisions. When we say "Yes," we often feel we're committing to something we might regret. But "No" feels like a protection against making a mistake.

Voss even trains salespeople to reframe their questions so that prospects say "No" in a way that moves the conversation forward. For example:

- Instead of "Do you want to save money?" ask "Would you like to spend more money than you need to?"
- Rather than "Are you interested in improving your home?" try "Would it be a bad idea to increase your home's value?"
- Instead of "Do you have time to talk?" ask "Is now a bad time to talk?"

In each case, saying "No" actually aligns with what the salesperson wants.

Now think about this in the context of parenting. When you say "No" to your child, you're not just setting a boundary—you're demonstrating strength, courage, and conviction. You're showing them that some things are so important that they're worth standing firm on. Kids need to see this from their parents. They need to know that mom and dad aren't pushovers who can be swayed by whining or tantrums. They need to see that you have the courage to stand up for what's right, even when it's hard.

But we can also apply Voss's strategy directly to parenting. Here are some ways you can use the "No" strategy with your kids:

1. Bedtime: Instead of "Is it time for bed?" try "Do you want to be really tired and exhausted before your big day tomorrow?"

2. Homework: Rather than "Do you want to do your homework now?" ask "Do you think it is wiser to do homework at the last second?"

3. Eating vegetables: Instead of "Will you eat your broccoli?" try "Do you think your body doesn't need good nutrients? "

4. Cleaning up: Rather than "Can you tidy your room?" ask "Do you want to sleep in a filthy room that stinks? "

5. Screen time limits: Instead of "Should we turn off the TV now?" try "Do you think it's good for your brain to stare at a screen for hours?"

Admittedly, some of the examples I gave for parents are more antagonizing than Chris Voss would recommend using with a hostage. But parents can be more direct anyway. The point, however, is by framing questions this way, you're allowing your child to feel in control by saying "No," while actually guiding them toward the behavior you want. It's a subtle psychological trick that can make your child feel like they're making the decision, rather than just following orders.

Remember, though, that saying "No" isn't about being mean; it's about setting boundaries. It's about teaching your kids that the world doesn't revolve around them. This is a hallmark of the blue-collar mindset. The rural life and the work that goes with it often revolves around "No." From running a farm to fixing cars to baking bread for your family, boundaries must be firmly established. You can't simply do what you please. You are often greeted with various "Nos," and by developing and strengthening a blue-collar soul, you and your children will be able to face them with perseverance and patience. Studies show that children who hear "No" develop better impulse control and emotional regulation.[2] They're more resilient in the face of disappointment—a crucial skill in the real world.

But let's be real: saying "No" isn't always easy. It can be downright

2 Morris AS, Silk JS, Steinberg L, Myers SS, Robinson LR. *The Role of the Family Context in the Development of Emotion Regulation*. Soc Dev. 2007 May 1;16(2):361-388.

uncomfortable, especially when your kid is giving you those puppy dog eyes or throwing a full-blown tantrum in the middle of the grocery store. That's when you need to remind yourself why you're saying "No." You're not just denying them something they want in the moment; you're teaching them a life lesson about limits, self-control, and respect for authority.

Here's a tip: practice saying "No" firmly but lovingly. For example, when your child asks for ice cream with dinner, respond with something like, "No, you can't have ice cream for dinner. I love you too much to let you eat junk all the time." This approach communicates both your boundary and your care for their wellbeing. Or why not try something a bit silly. If your kid asks do something that you think is unwise or inappropriate, like go to a movie with raunchy content, you could say, "You know that I spell LOVE—N.O."

Parents, deal with your own discomfort. Your job isn't to be your child's friend; it's to be their parent. Sometimes that means being the bad guy. Embrace it. Saying "No" is an act of love because it shows your child that you care enough to set limits and guide them toward what's best for them.

When you say "No," you're also modeling how to make tough decisions with integrity. Your kids are watching you closely, learning not just from what you say but from how you handle yourself under pressure. Every time you stand firm on a boundary, you're teaching them that strength comes from conviction and that discipline is an essential part of love. Imagine yourself as Gandalf with his staff, yelling at the dark forces, "You shall not pass!" This is you—if you are a good and loving parent.

So, flex that "No" muscle with confidence. Your kids may not thank you now, but one day they'll look back and realize that every time you said "No," it was because you loved them enough to do what was right instead of what was easy. And by skillfully using the "No" strategy, you're not just setting boundaries—you're teaching your children valuable decision-making skills that will serve them well throughout their lives.

WHEN TIME-OUTS DON'T CUT IT: REAL CONSEQUENCES FOR REAL WORK

My cousin, Jack, is a craftsman with a fantastic talent and work ethic. Everyone loves Jack. And anyone would want to hire Jack. One day a few years ago, he was using a circular saw, took his mind off the task at hand for just a second, and cut into two of his fingers. A very serious surgery followed. Part of one finger is gone forever, and the other was reconstructed, but with limited mobility. It was a real tragedy for a guy in his early twenties. For a man who holds tools for a living, this was a threat to his entire career. But in Jack's usual fashion, he carried himself with grace and humor and perseverance. He got back on the job quicker than most would. We were all so proud of him.

The moral of the story is this: data analysists don't deal with serious, life-threatening consequences if they mess up on the job. Blue-collar folks do. You want your kid to have a consequence mindset like Jack does more than some data analyst does working remotely in Starbucks.

In the blue-collar world, actions have real, tangible consequences. A welder who doesn't follow safety protocols doesn't just get a slap on the wrist; they risk serious injury. A farmer who neglects their crops doesn't just get a time-out; they face a failed harvest. As parents raising kids with a blue-collar soul, we need to instill this understanding early on.

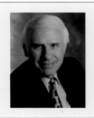

"Discipline is the bridge between goals and accomplishment."

–Jim Rohn

Time-outs might work for toddlers (though parents don't leave them in the corner nearly long enough for a bit of suffering to set in), but as your kids grow, you need to up your game. It's time for real consequences that teach real lessons—lessons that will serve them well in the practical, no-nonsense world of blue-collar work.

First, let's ditch the idea that discipline is some kind of cruel punishment, as if it is revenge for mom and dad. In the blue-collar world, it's about learning and improving. When you're designing consequences, ask yourself: What do I want my child to learn from this that will help them in the real world?

Here are some approaches to consequences, some of which have a blue-collar flair to them:

1. Natural Consequences:
   Let reality be the teacher when it's safe to do so. If your kid forgets their lunch, don't rush to school with it. A hungry afternoon might just teach them to be more responsible—just like a worker who forgets their tools can't do their job effectively.

2. Logical Consequences:
   These should mirror real-world outcomes. For example:
   • If your teenager misses curfew, have them research workplace punctuality and present on why being on time matters. (I remember my dad often had me do such research projects on the issue that I violated in my bad behavior. It was brutal, at least for a middle school kid that hated reading and writing.)
   • If your child doesn't do their chores, they don't get paid their allowance—just like not showing up for work means no paycheck.
   • If they're careless with tools, they lose the privilege of using them, mirroring how mishandling equipment on a job site has serious repercussions.

3. Restitution:
   In the blue-collar world, if you break it, you fix it. Apply this at home:
   • If they break something, they work to earn money to replace it or learn how to repair it themselves.
   • If they make a mess, they clean it up—no exceptions.

4. Added Responsibilities:
   Sometimes, the best consequence is more work. It builds character and work ethic:
   • Consistently late for school? They now have to get up earlier to do extra chores before leaving.
   • Didn't finish homework? They lose leisure time and instead help with household repairs or yard work.

Remember, one size doesn't fit all. What works for your eight-year-old won't work for your fifteen-year-old. Tailor your approach to each child's age and abilities, just like job responsibilities increase with experience:

For Young Children (5-8):
- Use a chore chart with rewards for completed tasks
- Short, work-oriented time-outs (like organizing a toolbox) or cleaning out the garage
- Loss of a privilege, replaced with a simple, helpful task

For Tweens (9-12):
- Loss of screen time, replaced with hands-on projects
- Extra chores that contribute meaningfully to the household (cleaning out stalls in our barn is a regular chore and/or punishment for this age group)
- Learning a new practical skill as a consequence

For Teens (13+):
- Loss of car privileges, coupled with learning basic auto maintenance
- Restrictions on social activities, replaced with internship-like responsibilities at home or in the community
- Increased responsibilities that mirror entry-level job tasks

Discipline takes creativity, mom and dad. You must get your executive hat on and get creative. When implementing consequences, be as consistent and no-nonsense as a good foreman. Follow through every time, or your words will lose their power, just like empty threats on a job site lead to chaos.

Always explain the consequence and its real-world parallel. For example: "Because you chose to stay out past curfew, you've shown you're not ready for that level of responsibility. In the real world, this could cost you your job. As a consequence, you'll be coming home an hour before curfew to do extra chores, so you learn that being on time is perfectly within your control." Pair consequences with guidance on better choices. The goal isn't just to correct bad behavior, but to build the reliability and work ethic prized in blue-collar fields.

Remember, we're not just raising kids; we're raising future workers, craftsmen, and responsible adults, whether they are carpenters or software engineers. A blue-collar spirit will help their white-collar career more than anything. By implementing thoughtful, consistent consequences that mirror real-world outcomes, you're preparing your children for success in the practical, high-stakes world of blue-collar work. It's not always easy, but neither is real work—and that's exactly the point.

> "A blue-collar spirit will help your kid's white-collar career more than anything."

UNITED WE STAND: PRESENTING A PARENTAL FRONT

Listen up, because this is crucial: you and your co-parent need to be on the same page. A house divided cannot stand, and neither can divided parents when it comes to discipline.

Consistency between parents or caregivers isn't just important—it's non-negotiable. Kids are smart. They'll exploit any crack in your united front faster than you can say, "But dad said I could!"

Sit down with your spouse and hash out your approach. Agree on the rules, the consequences, and how you'll enforce them. And for Pete's sake, don't undermine each other in front of the kids.

Got a disagreement? Take it behind closed doors. Present a united front to your children, even if you have to fake it till you make it.

CONCLUSION

Tough love with a tender touch. That's what you want.

In conclusion of this chapter all about discipline, let's talk about a discipline approach that's as practical as a well-stocked toolbox, but with the precision of a master craftsman: Love and Logic. This isn't some soft, feel-good nonsense. It's a no-nonsense way to raise kids who can handle the real world, while still showing them the compassion they need.

At its core, Love and Logic is about two things: showing your kids you love them fiercely and letting them face the music when they mess up. It's like teaching a kid to weld—you give them the right gear, show them how it's done, but then step back and let them learn from their mistakes. The key is to do it with a blend of firmness and tenderness.

HERE'S HOW IT WORKS IN THE TRENCHES:

Your kid forgets their lunch? Don't rush to school like their personal delivery service. Instead, you say with genuine concern, "Oh, man, that's rough. Being hungry at school is no fun. I feel for you. What's your plan to handle this?" Then zip it. Let them figure it out. You've shown compassion, but you're still letting them face the consequences.

The beauty of this approach is it teaches kids to think on their feet while knowing they have your support. It's not about you swooping in to fix everything; it's about them learning to handle whatever life throws at them, with the assurance that you're in their corner.

This method toughens kids up without breaking their spirit. It's like teaching them to change a tire—you show them how, offer encouragement when they struggle, but they need to get their hands dirty to really learn.

Love and Logic in action looks like this:

- When your kid complains about a tough teacher: "That sounds really frustrating. I'm sorry you're dealing with that. How are you planning to handle it? I'm here if you need to brainstorm ideas."
- If they're struggling with a project: "I can see this is really challenging for you. It's okay to find things difficult sometimes. What ideas have you come up with so far? I believe in your ability to figure this out."
- When they forget to do their chores: "Oh, no, I hate when that happens. I know you had plans, but those chores still need doing. How do you want to handle this?"

This approach isn't just about discipline; it's about raising kids who can hack it in the real world while knowing they have a safe place to land. Kids need to know how to solve problems, take responsibility, and not be afraid of hard work, but also know it's okay to struggle sometimes.

Remember, we're not raising kids; we're raising adults. Adults who can hold down a job, be reliable, and handle whatever curveballs life throws their way, but who also have the emotional intelligence to show compassion to others. Love and Logic helps build that grit and resilience our kids need, while also nurturing their hearts.

It's not always easy. Sometimes you'll want to step in and fix things. But stand firm, even as you offer comfort. Every time you let them solve their own problems while offering emotional support, you're building a stronger, more capable, and more empathetic adult. And in the end, isn't that what we're all aiming for?

A

BLUE-COLLAR SPIRIT WILL

HELP YOUR CHILD'S

WHITE-COLLAR **CAREER**

MORE THAN ANYTHING

5

REAPING THE REWARDS OF BLUE-COLLAR PARENTING

FROM CHORES TO CAREERS: SUCCESS STORIES THAT'LL MAKE YOU PROUD

Do you want to know if all this tough love, all these chores, all this blue-collar parenting actually pays off? First off, let me tell you about my own brood. I've got six kids old enough to work, and every single one of them has held down a job. Now, I'm not one to brag about my kids, but I've had the privilege of meeting every single one of their bosses—from the Whitewater Center to Chick-fil-A; from the local bagel shop to the grocery store. And you know what? Every single one of those bosses has looked me dead in the eye and said something along the lines of, "Man, your kids have the best work ethic. I wish all teenagers worked like yours. You've raised some hard workers!"

Now, don't get me wrong, my kids aren't perfect—far from it. But lazy? That's not in their vocabulary. And it's not by accident. Sure, having a houseful of kids means the older ones have to pitch in with the younger ones.

But we've been intentional—damn intentional—about holding our kids accountable for their actions, their chores, and their responsibilities. And let me tell you, it's paying off in spades.

But it's not just about flipping burgers or bagging groceries. This work ethic is showing up in their marriages, in figuring out how to raise a baby, in navigating the maze of buying a first house or dealing with insurance. It's about tackling life's challenges head-on, no matter what they are.

Now, as I mentioned in a previous chapter, I am also the CEO of a direct sales company. We've got people driving all over the country, knocking on doors to make sales. And you know who some of our best performers are? Farmers. That's right, we even had an Amish fella who left the farm and started selling for us. That farm work ethic? It translates beautifully into a white-collar sales job. They've got the discipline to get in and out of that car, day after day, no matter the weather or the rejections.

But here's where it gets really interesting. In my core business, TAN Books, a Catholic publishing company, we needed a new editor-in-chief. I got dozens of applications, all looking the same—theology degrees, literature degrees, the works. But one resume stood out like a sore thumb. This guy was a certified Ford mechanic. Before I even spoke to him, I thought, "Bet that's my guy."

Turns out, he was a Texas redneck, raised on a farm, grew up in a deer stand. He'd had a conversion experience, got some theological training, but didn't have much editorial experience. But you know what? I hired him. That's right, my editor-in-chief, my VP of Content for a conservative, traditional Catholic publishing company, is a certified Ford mechanic. To some, that might sound crazy. To me and my team, it makes perfect sense.

You see, we've got a blue-collar culture in our publishing company. Stuffy, ivory tower types don't last long here. But this Ford mechanic? He's been the best we've ever had in that position.

The bottom line? This blue-collar parenting approach? It works. It's producing kids who can hack it in the real world, who stand out from their peers, who know how to work hard and solve problems. And in a world that's getting softer by the day, that's worth its weight in gold.

So, keep at it, parents. Those chores, that discipline, that blue-collar mindset—it's setting your kids up for success in ways you can't even imagine. And trust me, the payoff is sweet.

BLUE-COLLAR SOUL IN A WHITE-COLLAR WORLD: THE COMPETITIVE EDGE

In my years of running businesses and participating in executive groups, one complaint consistently rises to the top: the difficulty in finding good workers. This isn't just the usual grumbling; in our digital age, especially post-Covid, it's become a genuine crisis.

The expectations of the younger generation entering the workforce are often unrealistic. They demand flexible hours, hybrid work scenarios, fully remote positions, rapid promotions, and high starting salaries. Many seem to lack the basic understanding that success requires putting in a full day's work, whether that's in a cubicle, making sales calls, or crunching numbers in the accounting department.

This is where blue-collar parenting pays dividends. Imagine a young employee who arrives at the office early, works diligently throughout the day, and doesn't expect constant praise for simply doing their job. This is what a blue-collar soul looks like in a white-collar setting. These individuals don't just meet expectations; they exceed them.

Good news for young employees: the bar has never been lower!

To be clear, I'm not against white-collar jobs. I have one myself, and most of my children will likely pursue similar paths. But I believe that even some of my children who choose blue-collar professions will likely end up running their own businesses, thus will be living in both the blue-collar and white-collar world. (By the way, beginning your career as a craftsman is an excellent way to become an entrepreneur.)

> "The greatest predictor of success is grit."
>
> —*Dr. Angela Duckworth*

The goal isn't to steer our children away from white-collar jobs, but to ensure they approach any job with a blue-collar mentality. Whether they end up in a prestigious law firm or a corner office in a skyscraper, that underlying grit and work ethic will serve them well.

There's a unique appeal to someone who can navigate the professional world with polish and articulation while also demonstrating the rigor and toughness that comes from a blue-collar background. Even in white-collar environments, there's an admiration for those who can combine professional demeanor with practical capability.

This combination of traits is increasingly rare and valuable. It's seen in popular culture too, where we often romanticize self-reliance and practical skills. There's a primal respect for those who can thrive in challenging environments, whether that's in the wilderness or the corporate jungle.

By raising our children with a blue-collar soul, we're equipping them with a competitive edge that will serve them well in any career path they choose. It's about instilling values of hard work, resilience, and pride in a job well done. These qualities will set them apart in a world where such attributes are becoming increasingly scarce.

In essence, we're not just preparing our children for specific jobs; we're preparing them to excel in any environment. The blue-collar soul we're cultivating will be their secret weapon, allowing them to stand out and succeed in whatever field they choose to pursue.

THE GRATITUDE EFFECT: FORGING FAMILY BONDS THROUGH HARD WORK

One of the most profound rewards of blue-collar parenting is watching hard work transform entitlement into gratitude. In a world where kids are often handed everything on a silver platter, the simple act of earning what they have can spark a deep sense of appreciation. When children experience the effort it takes to grow their own food, clean up after themselves, or contribute meaningfully to the household, they begin to see the value in what they have—and in the people around them.

Hard work fosters genuine gratitude because it shifts the focus from what they *want* to what they *have*. A child who helps repair a broken fence or spends hours cleaning out the goat stall understands firsthand the labor that goes into maintaining a home. They begin to appreciate not only their possessions but also the people who work tirelessly to provide for them. Gratitude isn't something we can lecture into our kids; it's something they learn through experience.

So how do we cultivate this thankfulness in our children? Start by giving them real responsibilities—chores that matter, tasks that contribute to the family's well-being. Let them see how their efforts make a difference. When they complete a tough job, acknowledge their contribution and connect it to the bigger picture: "Because you helped clean out the chicken coop, we have fresh eggs for breakfast." Small moments like these build a foundation of gratitude.

Another powerful way to foster gratitude is by creating family traditions around work and responsibility. In our home, shared challenges—whether it's planting a garden, fixing a gravel road, or tackling yard work together—have become opportunities for bonding. These aren't just chores; they're moments where we come together as a family to accomplish something meaningful. The laughter, teamwork, and even occasional frustrations forge bonds that are stronger than any store-bought experience.

When families work together, mutual respect naturally grows. Kids begin to see their parents not just as authority figures but as teammates who are willing to roll up their sleeves and get dirty alongside them. And parents start to see their children as capable contributors rather than passive recipients. This mutual respect strengthens family relationships in ways that no amount of quality time on the couch ever could.

The long-term benefits of cultivating gratitude and shared responsibility are immeasurable. Grateful kids grow into grateful adults—people who value hard work, cherish relationships, and approach life with humility and appreciation. And families who bond through shared challenges build relationships that last a lifetime.

In a culture obsessed with ease and convenience, blue-collar parenting offers something countercultural but deeply rewarding: the chance to raise kids who aren't entitled but grateful; who don't shy away from hard work but embrace it; and who understand that family bonds are forged not in comfort but in effort, perseverance, and love.

RAISING THE BAR: CULTIVATING HAPPY, HOLY, AND HARDWORKING ADULTS

In a world where mediocrity often seems to be the standard, blue-collar parenting offers a path to excellence. By instilling a strong work ethic, resilience, and problem-solving skills in our children, we're not just preparing them for success—we're setting them up to outshine their peers in every aspect of life.

The competitive advantage of a strong work ethic cannot be overstated. In an era where many young people expect instant gratification and shy away from challenging tasks, a child raised with blue-collar values stands out like a beacon. They're the ones who show up early, stay late, and tackle the tough jobs without complaint. This isn't just about impressing bosses or climbing corporate ladders; it's about approaching life with a level of dedication and commitment that sets them apart in every arena. It is about being good stewards of the gifts God has given us.

Consider this: while their peers might be scrolling through social media or playing video games, your blue-collar kid is learning to change a tire, fix a leaky faucet, or tend to animals. These aren't just practical skills—they're building blocks of resilience and problem-solving ability. When faced with a challenge, these kids don't throw up their hands in defeat or look for someone else to solve it. They roll up their sleeves and get to work.

This resilience and problem-solving mindset are invaluable in a rapidly changing job market. The truth is, we can't predict what jobs will exist in 20 or 30 years. But we can be certain that those who can adapt, learn quickly, and tackle challenges head-on will always be in demand. By raising kids with a blue-collar soul, we're equipping them with the mental toughness and practical skills to navigate whatever changes come their way.

But let's be clear: our ultimate goal isn't just to raise hard workers. We're aiming higher—we want to raise happy, holy, and hardworking adults. This is where the real challenge of blue-collar parenting comes in. It's not enough to teach our kids to work hard; we need to show them how to find joy and meaning in their work.

Balancing work ethic with emotional well-being is crucial. We don't want to raise workaholics who burn out by 30. Instead, we're cultivating individuals who understand the satisfaction of a job well done, who can find purpose in their daily tasks, and who know how to rest and recharge when necessary. This balance is something many adults struggle with, but by modeling it from an early age, we give our children a head start.

Integrating faith and values into daily life is another cornerstone of raising happy, holy, and hardworking adults. In our family, work isn't just about productivity or earning money—it's a way to honor God and serve others. Whether it's tending to animals, helping a neighbor, or excelling in schoolwork, we teach our children that their efforts have spiritual significance. This perspective transforms mundane tasks into meaningful acts of service and devotion.

The connection between meaningful work and life satisfaction is profound. Study after study has shown that people who find purpose in their work—regardless of what that work is—report higher levels of happiness and life satisfaction. By teaching our children to approach all work, whether it's mucking out stalls or writing a report, with dedication and a sense of purpose, we're setting them up for fulfilling lives.

This approach to parenting isn't always easy. It requires consistency, patience, and a willingness to go against the cultural grain. While other parents might be focused on making their children's lives as comfortable as possible, we're intentionally introducing challenges and responsibilities. It might look strange to outsiders, but the results speak for themselves.

I've seen it in my own children and in countless others raised with these values. They're the ones who stand out in job interviews, who excel in their careers, who build strong marriages and families. They're the ones who can handle setbacks with grace and tackle new challenges with confidence. They're not just surviving in the world—they're thriving.

"We do not act rightly because we are excellent, in fact we achieve excellence by acting rightly."

–Plato

"All endeavor calls for the ability to tramp the last mile, shape the last plan, endure the last hours toil. The fight-to-the-finish spirit is the one characteristic we must possess if we are to face the future as finishers."

—Henry David Thoreau

But perhaps most importantly, they're the ones who understand that true happiness doesn't come from external success or material possessions. It comes from living a life aligned with their values, from contributing meaningfully to their communities, and from approaching each day with gratitude and purpose.

As parents, we can't control every aspect of our children's lives or guarantee their success. But by raising them with a blue-collar soul—with a strong work ethic, resilience, problem-solving skills, and a deep sense of purpose—we're giving them the tools they need to navigate life's challenges and find true fulfillment.

The world doesn't need more entitled, soft-handed individuals who crumble at the first sign of adversity. It needs men and women of character who aren't afraid of hard work, who approach life with grit and grace, and who understand that true satisfaction comes from giving their best in everything they do.

That's the ultimate goal of blue-collar parenting: to raise adults who are not just successful by worldly standards, but who are truly happy, holy, and hardworking. Adults who can look back on their lives with satisfaction, knowing they've lived with integrity, purpose, and a commitment to excellence.

It's a high bar, no doubt. But as blue-collar parents, we're not afraid of a challenge. We know that the effort we put in now—the consistent discipline, the teaching of practical skills, the modeling of hard work and faith—will pay dividends for generations to come.

So, let's raise that bar. Let's commit to parenting with purpose and conviction. Let's raise children who will not just fit into the world, but who will change it for the better. Because in the end, that's what blue-collar parenting is all about: shaping the next generation of leaders, innovators, and difference-makers who understand the value of hard work, the importance of character, and the true meaning of success.

CONCLUSION

It goes without saying, but parenting is no easy task. You can approach it from many different angles and carry different philosophies into it, but you can never come lightly to parenting. My hope is that this book helps you on your parenting journey. It doesn't have all the answers, it won't do the parenting for you, but perhaps it will help to light a fire; to help you rise up and get your kids (and yourself) on that path of hard work and developing your blue-collar soul.

In a world of entitlement, of self-made victims, and blaming everyone but yourself when things go wrong, nothing is more extraordinary than a person who can carry themselves with grace and grit, who can stand up against failure or frustration, and persevere through it.

It doesn't matter what career you choose, what college you go to, how much money you make, or how big your house is. None of that matters. What matters most is how well you can walk through the fire. If you've only cultivated a pampered mindset, a white-collar hubris, a soul of entitlement for your child, they are in for a major wake up call.

The things of this world are passing, material matter doesn't matter at all in the end. But when you can cultivate a mindset and spirit of hard work, of resilience and grit, you can carry grace in your days. And as I said before, every parent wishes their child to be successful. But the fact remains: A blue-collar spirit will help their white-collar career more than anything.

So, Mom and Dad, help your children to push themselves to their fullest limits. Help them learn how to access those reserve tanks of grit when the hard times come. Show them how to do the work themselves and relish in the fruits of their own labors. It's time to step back, Mom and Dad, and allow your kids to become resilient, holy, hard-working adults. As St. John of the Cross said, "The road is narrow. He who wishes to travel it more easily must cast off all things and use the cross as his cane."

It's time to help your children become who they were truly meant to be. It's time to help them learn perseverance and joy through hard work. It's time to cultivate their blue-collar soul amid a white-collar world.

IMAGE CREDITS

p. 6 Official portrait photograph of Ronald Reagan, 1981. https://en.wikipedia.org/wiki/File: Official_Portrait_of_President_Reagan_1981.jpg / Source: https://www.dodmedia.osd. mil/DVIC_View/Still_Details.cfm?SDAN=DASC9003096&JPGPath=/Assets/Still/1990/ Army/DA-SC-90-03096.JPG / Author: Michael Evans (1944–2005) / Licensing: Public domain, via Wikimedia Commons

p. 7 Maximilian Kolbe in 1936 / https://en.m.wikipedia.org/wiki/File:Fr.Maximilian_Kolbe_ in_1936.jpg / Source: http://santuarioeucaristico.blogspot.hu/2010/08/sao-maximiliano-kolbe-14-de-agosto.html / Author: Unknown / Licensing: Public domain, via Wikimedia Commons

p. 9 The inner child and the inner parent illustration © luboffke, Shutterstock.com

p. 12 Las Meninas, https://en.wikipedia.org/wiki/File:Las_Meninas,_by_Diego_Vel%C3% A1zquez,_from_Prado_in_Google_Earth.jpg / Artist: Diego Velázquez (1599–1660) / Collection: Museo del Prado / Source/Photographer: The Prado in Google Earth: Home - 7th level of zoom, JPEG compression quality: Photoshop 8 / Licensing: Public domain, via Wikimedia Commons

p. 21 The Roaring Lion, Winston Churchill / https://en.wikipedia.org/wiki/File:Sir_ Winston_Churchill_-_19086236948.jpg / Photographer: Yousuf Karsh (1908–2002) / Collection: Library and Archives Canada / Source: Flickr: Sir Winston Churchill / Author: Yousuf Karsh. Library and Archives Canada, e010751643 / Licensing: Public domain, via Wikimedia Commons / Creative Commons Attribution 2.0 Generic (CC BY 2.0): https://creativecommons.org/licenses/by/2.0/deed.en

p. 27 Vince Lombardi statue in Green Bay, WI / https://commons.wikimedia.org/wiki/File: Vince_Lombardi_statue_in_Green_Bay,_WI.jpg / Source: https://www.flickr.com/photos/ jamiedfw/3425524456 / Author: Jim Bowen / Licensing: Public domain, via Wikimedia Commons / Creative Commons Attribution 2.0 Generic (CC BY 2.0): https://creative commons.org/licenses/by/2.0/deed.en

p. 33 Jesus helping St. Joseph in his workshop, Church of St. Joseph, Nazareth, Israel / Credit: G. Dagli Orti / © NPL - DeA Picture Library / Bridgeman Images

p. 39 Henry Ford / https://commons.wikimedia.org/wiki/File:Henry_Ford_portrait_1915_cropped. png / Source: The Henry Ford Collections, Object ID: 64.167.833.P.2973 / Author: Ford Motor Company. Photographic Department / Licensing: Public domain, via Wikimedia Commons

p. 42 Detail of the statue of the emperor Marco Aurelio at the Capitoline Hill in Rome, Italy © Anticiclo, Shutterstock.com

p. 44 Timer, clock, stopwatch by Hasan Sumon / social media logos by webhazrat / cell phone by Image Nest / kids on seesaw by Jovanovic Dejan / goldfish by Digital Bazaar © Shutterstock.com

p. 45 TV with remote control icon by fad82 / cell phone by Image Nest / Human head with Brain silhouette by chaiyo12 / sad emoticon by stas11 / video game controller by Nsit © Shutterstock.com

p. 51 Origen, portrait by Guillaume Chaudière (1584) / https://commons.wikimedia.org/wiki/File:Origen.jpg/Source:https://el.wikipedia.org/wiki/%CE%91%CF%81%CF%87%CE%B5%CE%AF%CE%BF:Origen.jpg / Licensing: Public domain, via Wikimedia Commons

p. 57 Frank Herbert / https://commons.wikimedia.org/wiki/File:Frank_Herbert_1984_(square).jpg / Source: https://www.ebay.com/itm/194862404422 / Author: Unknown photographer / Licensing: Public domain, via Wikimedia Commons

p. 64 Jim Rohn / https://commons.wikimedia.org/wiki/File:Jim_rohn.jpg / Source/Author: Tajul Islam Apurbo / Licensing: Creative Commons Attribution-ShareAlike 4.0 International (CC BY-SA 4.0): https://creativecommons.org/licenses/by-sa/4.0/deed.en

p. 77 Plato, detail of The "School of Athens" / https://commons.wikimedia.org/wiki/File:Sanzio_01_Plato_Aristotle.jpg / Artist: Raphael (1483–1520) / Collection: Apostolic Palace / Source/Photographer: Web Gallery of Art: https://www.wga.hu/art/r/raphael/4stanze/1segnatu/1/athens1.jpg / Licensing: Public domain, via Wikimedia Commons

p. 78 Farmer carrying a sack of potatoes on his shoulder © StockMediaSeller, Shutterstock.com

p. 4 (Sample Chapter) Portrait of William Shakespeare (1611) / Artist: John Taylor / National Portrait Gallery, https://en.wikipedia.org/wiki/File:William_Shakespeare_by_John_Taylor,_edited.jpg / Source, Photographer: https://www.npg.org.uk/collections/search/portrait.php?search=ap&npgno =1&eDate=&lDate= / User:Dcoetzee / Licensing: Public domain, via Wikimedia Commons

p. 6 (Sample Chapter) p. 6 Four-step process chart © Artos, Shutterstock.com

p. 13 (Sample Chapter) Narcissuss, circa 1600/ Artist: Caravaggio (1571–1610), https://en.m.wikipedia.org/wiki/File:Narcissus-Caravaggio_(1594-96)_edited.jpg / Source, Photographer: Hohum / Collection: Galleria Nazionale d'Arte Antica / Licensing: Public domain, via Wikimedia Commons

p. 15 (Sample Chapter) G. K. Chesterton(1909) / Photographer: Ernest Herbert Mills, https://commons.wikimedia.org/wiki/File:Gilbert_Chesterton.jpg / Source: National Portrait Gallery: https://www.npg.org.uk/collections/search/portrait.php?search=ap&npgno=x-134952&eDate=&lDate= / Licensing: Public domain, via Wikimedia Commons

p. 17 (Sample Chapter) The Tower of Babel (oil on panel) / Scorel, Jan van (1495-1562) / Netherlandish / Photo credit Cameraphoto Arte Venezia / Bridgeman Images

p. 18 (Sample Chapter) Saint Francis de Sales, https://commons.wikimedia.org/wiki/File:Saint_Fran%C3%A7ois_de_Sales.jpg / Source: http://www.santosebeatoscatolicos.com/2015/01/sao-francisco-de-sales-bispo-e-doutor.html / Author: Unknown / Licensing: Public domain, via Wikimedia Commons

RECOMMENDED READING

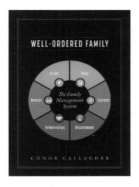

Well-Ordered Family:
The Family Management System
by Conor Gallagher

Do you yearn for more order and clarity within your family? Is the chaos and busyness of modern life unsettling the harmony of your household? Conor Gallagher, CEO of multiple businesses and father of fifteen, unveils a transformative system in Well-Ordered Family that will restore peace and joy in your household.

In his proprietary system, Conor has applied best business practices to the challenges of family life. The Well-Ordered Family Management System™ is broken down into six parts:

- **Vision:** Establish a clear path forward for your family, crafting a vision statement and defining your long-term goals.
- **Unity:** Institute a cadence of family meetings to help the family stay aligned around a shared vision.
- **Systems:** Implement effective macro and micro systems, creating environments and routines that foster efficiency and harmony.
- **Metrics:** Track and manage vital aspects of family life with simple, non-intrusive metrics that drive positive change.
- **Relationships:** Understand and leverage individual temperaments for stronger, healthier connections.
- **Discernment:** Use decision-making and problem-solving tools to guide your family through the daily challenges of life.

Packed with more than twenty-five practical tools, including worksheets and sample processes, Well-Ordered Family is a compass for families to reclaim order and clarity. Discover how business principles can revolutionize family life.

Join Conor Gallagher on this transformative journey to create a well-ordered family—because the grace you seek starts with the order you build.

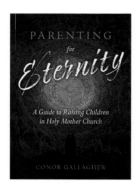

Parenting for Eternity:
A Guide to Raising Children in Holy Mother Church
by Conor Gallagher

A trillion years from now, your child will be either in Heaven or in Hell. And this is only the beginning of eternity.

In light of this eternal perspective, the time is now, Dear Parent, to raise your child to live entirely for Christ and His Church. The time is now to train your child in the Four Last Things, the spiritual life, the virtues of piety and humility, and the school of Calvary while shielding him from the errors of modernism, Protestantism, and much more.

Unlike most parenting books which focus exclusively on the body and this fleeting world, this short work focuses upon your child's eternal soul. In these pages, you will be challenged to see the eternal consequence of every single parental act—acts of commission and acts of omission.

The Lord has said unto you, it is better that you have a millstone hung around your neck and that you be cast into the depths of the sea than for you, Dear Parent, to lead your little one astray (Mk 9:41).

You Have Only One Problem:
Experience the Instant Reward of Trustful Surrender
by Conor Gallagher

You have a very big problem. Not a hundred, not dozens, not ten, but one—and it's a big one. Most of us put out fires on a daily basis, whether they be dirty diapers, bills to pay, car trouble, fractured familial relationships, or the dramas of your social circle. Our self-centeredness pulls us into these struggles and blinds our perspective to the greater truth that all of these stem from one core problem.

Perhaps the greatest misconception you carry in your mind and heart is that your suffering is bad or wrong or that it is in some other way a serious "problem." This little book will challenge that idea. It will help you see that, more often than not, your suffering is not your "problem" but a perfectly designed gift from God to bring you instant happiness.

So, what is your real "one problem"?

"Your one and only one problem is this: that you have not completely surrendered yourself and every part of your life to Divine Providence."

In *You Have Only One Problem*, Conor Gallagher, father of sixteen and CEO of TAN Books, takes you through an introspection that will change the way you approach the inevitable difficulties of life. This short book is easy to get through, but it is hard to read, for it pierces the soul with a straight edge on every page. With spiritual candor and frequent references to saintly examples, this book will make you stop and think about your sufferings in a completely new way. It will enable you to accept your joys and sorrows with the same frame of mind that countless saints have had before.

Trustfully surrendering to Our Lord is the only way to have no problems in this life. You cannot surrender 80 percent of yourself or 90 percent. You have to fully and completely surrender to Divine Providence—100 percent. Only then will you see all your perceived problems as they truly are: sanctifying gifts for your salvation. You will finish this little work with a perspective that can be perfectly summed in this simplest of prayers: *Lord, I wish to only wish what you wish.*

You are Never Too Busy:
Seeing Your Time the Way God Sees Your Time

by Conor Gallagher

What if you could never be "busy" again?

You always feel busy, with your to-do lists and packed calendars. There are kids' baseball practices, work lunches, sales presentations, home projects, and monthly bills. The list goes on and on and always will.

Upon reflection, you might admit that you take a little pride in how busy you are. This is why the question "How you doing?" is so often answered with the single word "Busy!"

But as author Conor Gallagher says, "Being busy might not be what you think it is. It really means that you are, in a manner of speaking, lost or out of control. It means the world has more power over you than God does."

As a free human, you *always* have time—plenty of time—to do God's will. The reason you might not see this clearly is the secret sin of modern times; not the sin of pride, or lust, or gluttony, but the oft-overlooked sin of sloth. How ironic it is that the busy person is often really guilty of being slothful!

In this short book, Gallagher, father of sixteen and CEO of TAN Books, will have a lasting impact on you as you hustle and bustle your way through life. His words will calm you and refocus you on your deepest desire: to do God's will.

Anyone who suffers from the anxiety of a "busy" life needs to read this book. It will show you how the saints were never busy and help you eradicate busyness from your daily life. You will finally discover peace and serenity amidst the chaos of the modern world.

"You are about to begin your journey to total freedom of time. Your time belongs to you and God. No one else. His gift to you is to never be busy again."

Still Amidst the Storm:
A Family Man's Search for Peace in an Anxious World
by Conor Gallagher

The apostles are trapped in a mighty storm, their fishing boat on the brink of capsizing . . . and Jesus slept. This confused, scared, and even angered the apostles, who could not fight back the storm. But as always, Christ is our model.

In these modern times, we often find ourselves adrift in a storm of stress, anxiety, and chronic busy-ness. We all suffer from it. In these moments, it's easy to react like the apostles: to panic, to become angry, to be frightened.

But like Christ, we should strive to be still amidst the storm. Here, Conor Gallagher (as a father of 15, no stranger to life's chaos) helps you reflect upon and cultivate three remedies to the stress of modern life:

- encountering God in the present moment, which requires a stillness of mind, to remain in the moment instead of fretting over past mistakes or future anxieties
- listening to the voice of God, which can only be heard by blocking out the relentless noise of the world and calming our increasingly restless souls
- resting in serene stillness by resisting the stir-crazy spirit of the world and rejecting busy-ness for busy-ness's sake

In a world that constantly bombards us with noise, this little book offers a wealth of practical advice and real-world guidance on how to cut out stress, anxiety, and worry so that we may rest in the Lord and hear His voice, so that we may be *Still Amidst the Storm*.

The Architect: How to Start Building Your Family's Ecosystem
by Conor Gallagher

You have been blessed with being the leader of your family. You have been blessed to be the architect of your life.

How exactly does someone take on an identity or become something new? Where does someone begin building the life for their family they always dreamed of?

In a day and age where the world threatens to pull families apart, where relationships grow shallow, and the cultural mindset centers around self-interest, you might wonder: What can I do to help my family?

While many parents feel overwhelmed and helpless, Conor Gallagher reminds us that, with grace and grit, you must step up and lead your family. In this short, yet poignant and plain-spoken book, you will learn ways to free yourself from the stress and become the leader your family needs.

"You can't outsource the design of your family's ecosystem," Gallagher reminds us.

By building your family's life with intention and vision, aligning purpose with virtue, you can begin to shape a thriving life for your family. Because if you're not leading your family, someone else will.

So it's time to arise and begin. You are the architect. You are the master builder.

Raising Catholic Kids for Their Vocations
By John S. Grabowski, PhD, Claire Grabowski

A practical guide for parents who want to form their children in the faith.

The mission of every married couple is to generously welcome children as gifts from God...then what?

As any parent knows, raising children is beautiful, exhausting, and often bewildering. And then we have their vocations to think about. It's the job of parents to raise children who are able to cultivate the gift of Faith and really listen to what God is calling them to do with their lives.

While God gives all the grace and faith necessary to follow him, we parents are tasked with fanning the flames. To help our children turn the spark of faith into a fire of love for God.

As parents, we need to make our homes communities of prayer, service, and witness within the larger Body of Christ. Making these regular and ongoing practices within the life of their family is the most effective way for parents to form their children in the faith.

Of course, this is not always easy; that's why Claire and John Grabowksi have made this practical guide. This is not high philosophy or deep theology (though it is rooted firmly in Church teaching) but real advice from real parents who have raised five children.

As parents, it's our job to get our children to heaven, and helping them discern the vocation God is calling them to is one of the most important parts of that job. You don't have to do it alone, with fervent prayer, a close relationship with Christ, and the tested, practical advice in Raising Catholic Kids for Their Vocation, you'll have the tools you need.

AN EXCERPT FROM
ANOTHER BOOK
IN THIS SERIES...

A
Well-Ordered Family
Short Read

THE ARCHITECT

How to

START BUILDING

Your Family's Ecosystem

CONOR GALLAGHER

CONTENTS

CHAPTER

1

BE THE HERO,
NOT THE VICTIM

The late American author and professor Joseph Campbell dedicated much of his career to studying and analyzing ancient literature and mythology. In his studies, he uncovered certain recurring patterns, ideas, and truths that lie at the heart of some of our most beloved stories and poems. But one quote that is particularly striking is about what it means to be a hero. Campbell wrote, "Your life is the fruit of your own doing. You have no one to blame but yourself." And elsewhere he wrote, "The big question is whether you're going to be able to say a hearty yes to your adventure."

Stories of myths and heroes have permeated our human identity since time out of mind. From epic poems and hieroglyphics to binge-worthy Netflix shows and comic books, we as a culture have long admired ordinary people placed in extraordinary situations. Our hearts race and we bray with elation when good triumphs over evil.

We long to be that hero. We long for the courage to overcome adversity and sorrow.

"Some are born great, some achieve greatness, and some have greatness thrust upon them."

—*William Shakespeare*

For the past fifty years or so, however, I would argue that we've buried such courage. We've sadly exchanged our role of aspiring to great virtue with self-pity. We've become self-made victims in a cruel world. But saddest of all is that this has become an accepted norm for many of us.

Now, what is this self-victimization? The simple definition is self-victimization is the tendency of individuals to perceive themselves as victims, attributing their problems and misfortunes to external factors rather than acknowledging their own responsibility. Why would someone want to do this? Because they desire sympathy, compassion, and frankly, a free hand out. They want someone to take the blame so they don't have to take responsibility for working hard, overcoming obstacles, and winning on their own merits. In our super-sensitive world, if you are a victim, others will take care of you. If you are a victim, you are entitled.

This cycle of self-made victims has become a virus within our culture. It's a psychological parasite that's spreading rampantly through this modern age. This isn't completely ridiculous though. In fact, it's quite understandable that this would happen in a culture filled with spoiled rotten brats. And remember: it doesn't take money to be spoiled rotten. My kids have grown up with plenty of money, but they are not spoiled in the least. (They have their issues but being spoiled ain't one of them.) With the number of kids in our family, they have been forced to work things out, to deny self, to help others when it is highly inconvenient. Even if you are poor, you have the ability to spoil your kids rotten by the way you raise them. We aren't talking money; we are talking how you raise your kids to be accountable for their own actions.

A story just from the other night may illustrate the point. We were watching the Yankees and Dodgers in the 4th game of the World Series. Imelda (12) went outside to get something from the refrigerator (the extra one) and a large glass bottle of sparkling water fell out of the fridge, shattering on the garage floor. A huge mess. Tons of little shards of glass. Water everywhere. She came inside and told me. I asked her if she was capable of cleaning up the mess or if she needed me. She said she could do it, albeit a little reluctantly, hoping I might take the burden from her. She asked her brother David (11) for help. He willingly left the game and helped her.

Now, I went outside to check on them three or four times and would have of course intervened if they needed help. But they handled it. They even moved the fridge in order to get the shards of glass that shattered beneath it. I saw little David pushing that fridge with his back, feet up against the water heater giving him leverage. It was a funny sight. It took at least thirty minutes, missing much of the game.

I think most parents would have done the clean up for them, or, had to force a much older sibling to help. I was so proud to see my kids handle such a big mess together. This, my friends, is why my kids end up being excellent employees: they know how to work. They are not the victims of a broken bottle. Rather, they were heroes that solved the problem.

Now, there are many factors and situations that can lead to true, justified victimization. True oppression exists. Real suffering can strike and leave families devastated and ruined. But most people in our culture live with all the modern comforts this century has to offer. Sturdy houses and apartments with running water and electricity; every new piece of technology; all the streaming services; the fastest internet; food that can be delivered at any moment….This is an age of instantaneous abundance. Those that have it are sucked into it; those that don't have it long for it. It is a spoiled age obsessed with the material. It is a virtual age that despises the virtuous.

It's easy to imagine this spoiled brat on a micro level. You've seen it in movies, read it in novels, known some family that spoils their kids to death. That kid who has been spoiled is destined to see themselves as a victim of their circumstances. This is because they haven't had to persevere. They haven't had to fight through difficulty or truly yearn for something more. They simply complain about every meaningless frustration or things not going exactly as they wish.

My brother Brian makes this funny joke where he'll act like something's really wrong. I'll ask, "What's wrong, Brian?" He'll do this fake pouting cry and say, "My toaster doesn't have a bagel setting."

We have become self-made victims in many ways because our luxury cars don't pair with our smartphones, or our package won't arrive from Amazon instantly. We've lost sight of ourselves because we wallow in misfortune and blame others for it. We've shrugged off our great adventure and instead whine that we have to get off the couch.

YOU MUST BREAK THE CYCLE

The novelist G. Michael Hopf is credited with coining the saying, "Hard times create strong men. Strong men create good times. Good times create weak men. Weak men create hard times."

If you look back through American history (I'd argue back as far as the founding of any civilization) this has been humanity's cycle. It has been especially present in American culture since at least World War I.

Consider the generation that fought in World War I. The trench warfare was horrific and devastating. These young men came home from tragic battles and went to work, often very hard, manual labor jobs in factories, shipyards, or farms. They worked to build families and make lives after the war, and then the Great Depression struck. They didn't have any extended period of time of ease. These were hard times, to say the least. The Depression and post-war culture wreaked havoc in the country, but the people were tough, they persevered and never gave up.

The children that grew up in the Depression saw mom and dad fighting to have every little thing that they had. They learned to be grateful for what there was and work hard to get just a bit ahead. There was no room to become spoiled. These same children grew up and then went off to World War II themselves, already tough as nails from being Depression-era babies.

Those hard times in American society created strong men and women. They were strong from the Depression. They were strong from the war. They came back home, and wished to build strong lives, strong communities. They built factories and businesses. And through all of this, these strong men and women created good times.

As a result of their hard work, there came a boom in America. Throughout the 50s, 60s, and 70s, technology and industry soared. New homes were built, mass manufacturing made life easy and made necessities easily accessible.

But the next generation, the "baby boomers," disrupted much of this. My father is a quintessential baby boomer, born in 1950. When he turned 18 or 19 years old, what was going on in America? It was the sexual revolution. Woodstock and long hair. Suddenly, it's the anti-war movement, anti-patriotism, race wars. Some things improved, but many things began to fall apart, and major division entered society in unprecedented ways. The age of entitlement began.

MACRO CAUSES OF A VICTIM MINDSET

Mindsets changed in such drastic ways in a short amount of time. No longer was focus placed on family or communities or even a country, but instead it was shifted to the individual. JFK's famous line, "Ask not what your country can do for you, but what you can do for your country," was a prophetic warning of the upside-down mindset becoming prevalent. Ever since that baby boomer generation, the mindset has been "What can my country do for me?"

Advertising became aimed at the individual. Music and television provided narratives of self-centeredness. And at the same time, there was no longer worry or need to have a family or remain chaste, because the invention of "the pill" brought a new form of sexual freedom. Suddenly men and women become spoiled in a whole new way because there were no consequences to their sexual deviancy.

Babies became commodities. Families became customers. War became an industry because it was good for the economy.

So, in post-war America, these strong men and women made good times. My father's generation grew up in the good times, but those times created weak men and women.

Politically, this baby boomer generation embraced big government. With welfare and social programs holding over from the post-Depression years, what was supposed to be momentary relief for a devastated country became a foothold for power hungry politicians. The philosophy of the 60s was one of radical individualism. It should come as no surprise that a spirit of entitlement possessed our nation.

You can even see this weak-men-mentality manifesting itself in economic policy of "big government's going to have to take care of us." No longer was there a pride of place, of ownership, or community. Mindsets became "what can they do for *me*?"

MAKE YOUR KIDS CLEAN UP THE BROKEN GLASS

Those good times created these weak men and women. These weak men and women created an economic policy of entitlement and victimization. While welfare and social support for the poor is needed, big government used such programs to essentially victimize the populace, divide races, knowing that they could continually be put in office and elected when they promised to make things better and give things away. It became a game of weakening already weak people, promising to help but doing nothing in the end. And that dynamic is still going on politically and economically. Perhaps this was no better demonstrated than upon Barack Obama's election when people literally started asking, "Where's my new car?"

If you make the people weak, they will always need you. It's a constant circle of taking out legs from under people so that they must lean on someone else. Such a government and cultural zeitgeist becomes a tyrant, posing as savior.

> "No one can make you feel inferior without your consent."
> *–Eleanor Roosevelt*

This weak generation has been in charge for a long time and has continued to feed this cycle of victimization. The baby boomers are in their seventies and beginning to retire now. But they have created a weak generation, and thus we are on the threshold of hard times. The cycle continues on.

Another striking theory poses a similar kind of cycle. Throughout history, nations have gone through a cycle of peace and war, peace and war. If you look at a generation that's in the war, they witness firsthand the devastation and horrors of war. There is nothing romantic about it.

Those people go back home, take on political offices, and they don't want to go to war again. They know what it's like, so they strive for peace. Generation two, their children, watched dad come home broken and traumatized. They heard the horror stories of war. So, they too promote peace.

But then generation three, the grandchildren, came along and didn't grow up with the sense of war. They didn't have a close connection and or see grandpa's PTSD. This generation thinks these policies of peace are silly and unnecessary. Without that terror of war, they begin to lead the country down dangerous paths and soon enough back to war again[1].

---

1 The Strauss–Howe generational theory, also known as the Fourth Turning theory, was developed by William Strauss and Neil Howe and outlined in their 1997 book "The Fourth Turning: An American Prophecy."

The theory proposes a recurring generational cycle in American history, consisting of four turnings that repeat every 80-100 years: High (First Turning); Awakening (Second Turning); Unraveling (Third Turning); Crisis (Fourth Turning). According to this theory, each turning lasts about 20-25 years, and the cycle is driven by generational archetypes that react to the previous generation's excesses. The generation that experiences a major crisis or war (Fourth Turning) emerges with a desire for stability and peace. Their children, raised in the aftermath, continue to value peace and institutions. Grandchildren begin to question the established order. Great-grandchildren come of age during a time of crisis, potentially leading to another major conflict.

I think we're at a time where our country has experienced a long time of peace. We've had war in the Middle East and various countries, of course, but we have not had an all-out war like Vietnam or WWII. The general population has had a generous gap between such horrific violence. We don't have a cultural memory of the horrors of war. We do things that will jeopardize our peace and throw ourselves back in war, beginning right here in our own society.

Such paradigms only go to show we are in a wimpy era. Not that we need war or a Great Depression to make us strong, but we must pass on the virtues that come with perseverance through sorrow. We must uphold human dignity in order to break these cycles.

In short, we are a spoiled generation, one that has been spared the atrocities of war and have drowned in a tsunami of abundance.

Dear parents, the culture will not make your child tough; it will make your child weak. Making them tough is up to you. And this is not done by making your kid pump iron in the garage, but by making them clean the broken bottle in the garage. This is done by creating an environment of accountability, self-reliance, and grit.

A SPOILED MINDSET

The dawn of extraordinary technology has only further propelled our spoiled and corrupted dispositions. We no longer suffer in the same ways as previous generations, which is a blessing, but we suffer differently. We have severe poverty, but it is a different type of poverty.

Now, spoiled can take on many meanings. While a great many of us have been materially spoiled, I think it is more of an entitled mindset. Whether or not we have luxury cars or iPhones, our society tells us that we *must* have it, that we *deserve* it. This is our spoiled nature; this leads us into becoming self-made victims, demanding that we deserve.

As I mentioned earlier, if you're a spoiled brat in a mansion, it's somewhat easy to see that your life crumbles when somebody doesn't make the shrimp cocktail the way you like it. Of course, it's silly and absurd, but you can see that kid melting down and say, well, no wonder. We can stand back with smug hauteur at such a scene, but the reality is we would all act totally spoiled if we were all totally spoiled. We wouldn't know otherwise. And this is the case now. Culturally, we're spoiled in unprecedented ways.

Not only are we following the typical cycle and entitled mindset, but we really do have a material abundance that the world has never seen. Mass production of food, clothing, shelter, and technology, everything, and quite literally everything, is at our fingertips, just a click away.

THE DAYS OF OUR LIVES

So, how and where does this self-victimization begin? I would argue it is generally within our control. We cast ourselves into the role of a victim. Perhaps society at large initiated it, but we perpetuate it.

Think of a teenage girl who has sat and watched endless amounts of dramas on T.V. Every good story has a certain story arc to it. There's the situation and drama, there's a villain and the hero. The hero somehow becomes a victim and must overcome some feat in order to restore things back to how they should be, often much better than before. We've all seen this story. There are only a few basic storylines that are repeated time and again, after all.

Romeo and Juliet has been retold a million times. *The Lord of the Rings*, *Star Wars*, and *The Matrix Trilogy* all have basically the same premise of "the chosen one." A drama builds on itself with situation after dire situation until the tension is almost unbearable.

In this example, this teenage girl has seen all of these dramas countless times in every T.V. show and movie she's ever watched. Her whole cultural worldview is based on this drama. And every good drama has to have some kind of sacrificial victim, has to have some kind of bully. It's hard to be redeemed if you're not a victim, after all. And because society has done away with a sense of the true victim, which was us as a result of Original Sin and our need of a true redeemer, Jesus Christ, this teenager is left searching for that dynamic to be present in her life.

Such people place themselves in the movie. They place themselves in the T.V. show and they cast themselves as the victim. They want to be in the reality show or the soap opera, they want to be the hero with the horse or the beautiful couple getting married. This becomes almost a coping mechanism.

They do have legitimate problems. They have broken families, live in a crazed, manic society, and are bombarded with the world 24/7.

The social environment that they're being raised in, along with the technological environment, the religious environment, the recreational environment, the educational environment, and the professional environments, those six environments (we'll talk about these in more depth in later chapters) are really harsh environments for most people. They have not been built to foster a sense of peace and security, but rather isolation and anxiety. So, becoming a victim is a natural consequence.

This isn't entirely their own fault either. There's certainly legitimacy to this. But there is also a clear manipulation at play. This victimization is a manipulation of others, veiling truth and telling them they have nowhere else to turn. It turns attention entirely to self and self-interest.

> "True heroism is remarkably sober, very undramatic.
> It is not the urge to surpass all others at whatever cost,
> but the urge to serve others at whatever cost."
>
> —Arthur Ashe

Much like the Greek myth of Narcissus, the beautiful young man who falls so deeply in love with his own reflection in the water that he falls in and dies, we too have become obsessed with our own reflections.

With social media, with the way our school systems and sports teams work, the world has become a mirror. Everywhere you look, every environment that you're going into, it requires people, particularly young people, to be extremely self-conscious of how they look, what are they wearing, how they're performing, what they are saying, what group are they in. Of course, these sorts of social hierarchies have been present in society throughout history to some extent. Even the ancient Romans had hierarchies of greater togas and lesser togas (the cool kids wore nicer togas, of course).

We've now reached an all-time high where the styles and fads change so rapidly, and there are abundant resources to buy and adopt new fads so

Narcissus. Circa 1600, Caravaggio.

quickly that just to keep up with it is almost impossible. We're endlessly look-ing at ourselves, weighing, measuring, analyzing, just to make sure we're up to date and not left behind. It's constant. And there's so much abundance that it is impossible to keep up. We have so much "stuff" we think is so important. And when we don't have it, all we can do is obsess over getting it.

We've become spoiled to the point of believing our happiness and peace lies in getting what we want, and not what we need. We're spoiled to the point where we're bubbling over with pride and self-interest. It's purely a spoiled culture and its yolk is too much to bear.

YOUR BURDEN OF ABUNDANCE

The biggest problem with this self-victimization is that parents are adopting this troublesome notion at alarming rates.

Parents, especially younger parents, have grown up in this spoiled culture. They've grown up with total abundance (again, not only material, but in self-serving entitlement too) and it has become a great burden. Tremendous abundance is a very difficult thing to bear.

Imagine two hikers set out through the forest on a long journey. The first thinks of everything. In his pack he has a tent, plenty of high-quality food, extra pairs of clothing, pans, dishes, a little fan in case it's hot, lawn chair in case he wants to rest. He has everything with him on this long and treacherous journey, but it weighs him down. He grows more and more tired, having to stop and rest. His legs are ready to give out not even halfway through the journey. He has never been taught how to pack lean. He thinks that all of this garbage that he's carrying is necessary to survive. While at the same time, the second guy on the other trail has brought only the bare essentials. He has a small backpack and only brought what he truly needed, and he's getting through the journey so much better.

You can look at these two people and feel sorry for the idiot who is burdened because everyone told him, "Don't forget to bring your extra neck pillow." He's helplessly burdened by abundance.

Parents today feel helpless in similar ways. They feel they are victims, and you can see that parents have adopted this psychosis of self-victimization. They have a middle schooler and a high schooler, and they are so completely and totally overwhelmed.

Why? Well, there are a number of reasons. But whether it's kids in sports, both spouses having to work two jobs just to pay all the bills, keeping up with teachers at school, keeping up with the house and cars and all the day-to-day struggles, it quickly feels like you're treading water but never making it to the shore. As they grow more exhausted by the spinning world, the constant demands on them from their kids, friends, family, people slip right back into this mindset of feeling like that can't break out. They'll never get ahead; they'll never find peace. This turns into blaming everyone but themselves, and they are playing victim once again. Why? Because it's always easier to blame someone, something else than to pull yourself up and start changing your life.

So many people feel they must be perfect and do extraordinary at everything. They must work hard to move up in work, while being a perfect spouse, perfect parent, and they must be improving themselves and upgrading their life all the time. The mindset of perfection and abundance surrounds you. It's an exhausting system that traps you and makes you feel like there's no way out.

"The most extraordinary thing in the world
is an ordinary man and his ordinary wife
and their ordinary children."

–G.K. Chesterton

I think this abundant, busy mindset is a major culprit for making parents feel like victims. That recreational environment takes a ton of time. I remember when we were a big-time baseball family, and we had five kids on four different baseball teams at once. I certainly felt helpless. It was constant and all-consuming. The idea of my boys not playing little league baseball was anathema. So, we had to start making some tough decisions. We decided to take one season off from little league. And we never went back. These days, we wait much longer until our kids get into organized sports. Admittedly, I have 16 kids. So my situation is a little more complex than the average family. But I wish I had considered this much earlier than I had. Even with five kids, we were spinning out of control. We needed to slow down, but I was scared to do so. I wanted to "feel" like a good dad taking my kids to the field every day. Now, I'm focused on being the architect of an incredible ecosystem that provides what my kids really need to become virtuous, competent, and tough as hell.

The key thing is that these parents feel helpless because they are allowing the culture to build their infrastructure, their ecosystem, as opposed to the parents themselves building the ecosystem.

I'm not against sports. I'm not against kids playing instruments. I'm not against kids doing ballet. I'm not against vacations or any of that stuff. But parents today must remember that if the history of humanity was a 24-hour clock, kids have been playing organized sports for 20 seconds. (I did the math.[2])

It is remarkable how parents have adopted extraordinary convenience and luxury things that we have, such as organized sports, as absolute necessities for well-being. It's something that just walked on to the stage of humanity, and we assume that it's absolutely necessary to fulfill a thriving life. Parents allow the culture to build their life. Parents allow culture to be the architect of their family and they're too weak to stand up and do something about it. This is a major problem.

> "You live in a deranged age, more deranged than usual because, in spite of great scientific and technological advances, man hasn't the faintest idea of who he is or what he is doing."
>
> —*Walker Percy*

When someone else is the architect and forces you to go this way and that, and you have to do this and you have to do that, you have to buy these clothes, you have to drive this car, your kids have to do these activities, you have to live according to the standard—of course you will feel like a victim.

---

2 300,000 years of human history = 24 hours
- 1 hour = 12,500 years
- 1 minute = 208.33 years
- 1 second = 3.47 years

Now, let's calculate how many seconds 70 years represents:
70 years ÷ 3.47 years/second = 20.17 seconds

Therefore, if the entire 300,000-year history of humanity were compressed into a 24-hour clock, the last 70 years would represent approximately 20 seconds.

The Tower of Babel. Scorel, Jan van (1495-1562)

In a sense, you are a victim, but you allowed yourself to become one, and you allow it to continue. And remember, this sense of self-victimization is a choice. It's a mindset we've adopted. It can absolutely change, but that requires change from you.

So, do you have the guts to say no, mom and dad? Can you say, "I'm not going to let this culture dictate how my family is built. I'm going to build it myself."

YOUR FALSE FEAR OF FAILURE

Parents also feel like victims because they feel like there's nothing they can do about it. And the reality is that this is a devastatingly shortsighted sense of their own creative powers to build a family that they choose to have.

For some reason, when people build a business, they're much more creative. They often get excited and courageous, saying, "No, this is my business. I'm going to do it the way I want to do it."

They don't let the outside world dictate to them their entrepreneurial efforts. People are far more independent and autonomous and creative and imaginative and resilient against external pressures when it comes to entre- preneurship or creativity.

But when it comes to family, we just tuck our tails, fall in line, and do what we're told.

Why is this? We have a longing to be our own person. We have a longing to be creative and imaginative and innovative and strategic and to be different than our competitors. We have a family because we longed for one and were blessed with one. Yet every day, many of us do nothing to better our families.

Many people have an extreme sense of ownership over something they've made and don't want anyone else to mess it up. They're not afraid of their business or creative work standing up and walking away saying, "I don't like what you did with me." It's theirs. It came out of their creativity.

But kids do this every day. They stand up at some point in their life and say, "I'm done with you, dad and mom. I don't want you to be my dad any- more. I don't like what you've done." Spouses do this with each other, and it's terrifying.

"Nothing is so strong as gentleness; nothing so gentle as real strength."

–*St. Francis de Sales*

We've become conditioned to the falsehood that love and family and marriage are conditional. We cower when real conflict arises because we don't want to "lose" our kids or spouse. Or, on the other hand, we become overly aggressive and walk away ourselves, thinking we deserve better. But we don't work on fixing things when they're broken. We hide or walk away and allow something or someone else to take the lead.

How many parents have I met in my life that cannot bring themselves to discipline their children, particularly dads, because they are scared to death that their kid is going say, "Screw you. I'm out." Especially when they're teenagers. They are scared to death that their teenage daughter is just going to get in her car and drive away.

This goes right back into playing victim. They say, "I'm helpless here. I can't even discipline my kid because everything's against me: my spouse, my kids, my job, culture...EVERYTHING!"

I see so many dads who are scared of their own children. And they love their children. They don't want their kids to leave. So, they compromise, and compromise and compromise and compromise. Thinking that that's going to keep them close, when in reality, it doesn't.

Instead, dad and mom must demand respect but also give affection.

I think we fall into a dichotomy of thinking we can only do one or the other. But you have to give both. You have every right to. God the Father wrote it in the Ten Commandments. Honor your father and mother.

You are owed respect from your children. And they are owed affection from you.

We get into this mode of playing victim because, on some level, we're afraid of failure. We're afraid to stand up and take the reins of our family because what if we screw up? What if something happens and everyone leaves? So, we just let others take the reins and we whine and complain and remain helpless.

But you must recognize this is a false sense of failure. You must see that the culture that you have grown up in has created a self-victimization psychosis, one that is stronger than ever before in human history. If you don't recognize it, you can't fight it.

Once you do recognize it, then you're able to say, "Ok, I'm not a victim. I'm the architect."